THE *Dream Dollhouse* DO-IT-YOURSELF BOOK

JULIE SHELTON

Postal: Pipkin Press, 330 St George's Rd, North Fitzroy, 3065, Victoria, Australia
Email: dreamdollhousediy@gmail.com
Visit DreamDollhouseDIY.com for more information

First published in Australia 2014
Copyright © Julie Shelton 2013
Cover design, book design, typesetting: Erin Hedrington, erinhedrington.com

Author: Shelton, Julie
Title: The Dream Dollhouse Do-It-Yourself Book : Adorable Goodies
          for the Fashion Dollhouse
ISBN: 9780987527004 (paperback)

Subjects: Miniature craft.
          Miniature objects.
          Dollhouses.
DDN: 745.5928

Disclaimer
Craft at your own risk. All care has been taken to ensure that the information in this book was correct at press time, but the author and publisher do not assume and hereby disclaim any liability to any party for any loss, damage, or disruption caused by errors or omissions, whether such errors or omissions result from negligence, accident, or any other cause. All contact details given in this book were current at the time of publication, but are subject to change.

The advice given in this book is based on the experience of the individuals. The author and publisher shall not be responsible for any person with regard to any loss or damage caused directly or indirectly by the information in this book.

To Simon and Andrew, neither of whom has any interest in dolls.

Julie Shelton is a keen crafter with a lifelong love for 1:6 miniatures. She lives in Melbourne, Australia.

Erin Hedrington is a designer and kid at heart, intensely nostaligic about her doll-playing days. She lives in Chicago, Illinois.

Contents

Introduction

Living & Dining Room

Kitchen

Bedroom

Bathroom

The Dream Dollhouse
DO-IT-YOURSELF BOOK

Introduction

Lots of us have one. People tell me about them all the time. Under the bed. Or in the back of the closet. The box, the suitcase. Full of childhood memories and far too precious to ever, ever, throw out.

It might contain the dolls themselves, frizzy hairdos and all.

Or you might be lucky enough to have a really stylish stash. I have a friend who has a shoe box full of the sixties cotton clothes her mother made for her doll, sweetly detailed with darts and tiny buttons.

I wanted all the projects in this book to be both easy and adorable. To play with for hours with a sister or bestie. To live quietly in a cupboard at Grandma's until small people visit. To be discovered by a new generation who will be mystified by the odd stuff called plastic or plywood.

Most of all, to create those special memories of doing something magic with a treasured adult. The memories that sustain us when times are tough. Knowing that someone cared enough to do this with us, to share our small reality, to have the time and patience to make something just to amuse us, and perhaps to teach us some skills as well.

I wanted designs that are painless to make and don't need anything complex or expensive. I had an important test for these minis. It is a single question that I asked myself: "Do I want to make this again?" If the answer was "no", it didn't go into the book.

Fabric, paper, plywood, pre loved stuff, packaging, paint and glue. Optional power drill. No complex woodwork and no power saws.

They are quick to do, honest. Many of them are just things glued together. And what child will ever forget the day that Mummy and I made a doll sofa…or a tiny lamp… or a fairytale bed for that precious doll.

I like to use the objects we might usually throw out. Why not? Many are made of long lasting materials, they are budget friendly, and often free.

Ah, this book was such fun to do. These minis are both childhood fun and memories in the making. And I do hope that some will end up in that precious stash under the bed. ♥

Chapter One
The Goodies

The world is full of ordinary objects that can become something else entirely. Our own special version of upcycling. This book is not about starting from scratch. Oh, no, no, no. We want to have lots of the work done by somebody else. We just want to do the fun part.

Our materials are pretty simple. I don't like expensive specialist materials. And scavenging is a DIY activity in this book.

My favorite material is 3 ply sheet wood, because it can be cut with a craft knife. This is as close as we get to real woodwork. Plywood can be bought from ordinary hardware stores, or scavenged from picture frame backings and drawer bottoms.

Thick and thin cardboard is great when it will be covered up. Keep any pieces that come your way. You can also buy it from art supply stores, but they usually sell only in large sheets, which are surprisingly expensive.

For a dollhouse, the biggest impact is the fabric design, so a clever pick from your stash creates the room. Color is magic, and pink is still top choice. Fabrics that mimic full size designs are fun, like the duvet cover and pillows made for Bayo box bed (p. 56), which has a cool graduated design.

Hmm...maybe for my curtains?

If you like, lace and trims can be added in seconds with glue, and contribute major eye appeal.

Skewers, wire coathangers and toothpicks hold everything together. Ordinary bamboo skewers are about 3mm diameter and are quite strong. I cut them with my pliers. They paint well. Chunks of cork from champagne corks can add strength to joints too.

But this is not an excuse for hoarding. You are only making one dollhouse. Be very selective. Only shell out that dollar or two once you have made a conscious decision to transform that candleholder, picture frame, or box into something fabulous.

Fashion dolls are about one sixth the height of a real person. So these projects are 1:6 scale, which is often called playscale. Traditional dollhouses like Queen Mary's Dollhouse at Windsor Castle and the Thorne Miniature Rooms at the Art Institute of Chicago are half that size at 1:12 scale.

And here is list of 10 of my favorite upcycled goodies. These are the sweetheart bits and pieces that I hunt for when I am wearing my 1:6 playscale goggles.

So here they are. My all time faves. ♥

01 Picture Frames

Ah, so much fun. So cheap, cheap, cheap, once they have had their day in the homemaking fashion sun. Sturdy enough for lots of play, just the right size and so much detailing. And they come in great materials-wood, resin, plastic, metal. So easy to glue, paint, drill and so on.

You may never have thought about this, but frames have a back too, as well as their gorgeous fronts. And those backing pieces are rectangular machine cut pieces, often made of 3mm MDF or plywood, and made just the right size for us. See what I mean about somebody else doing the work?

I do like to be able to use both the frame and the backing. If they are both in usable shape that is a big plus. Never throw out the funny shaped props from the backs either; they are perfect paint stirrers.

So, what do I look for in a frame? Out of the hundreds of frames waiting to be taken home from my local op shops, which ones get to go into my reusable shopping bag? I have some favorites, and when I see them, my 1:6 goggles snap into instant focus.

The Chunky
Any frame with depth to it is a natural. Some are deep enough to make a coffee table base, for example. Chunkies can also become part of something else, like Tomasina table (p. 21).

The Transformer
This is the frame that has the right detailing at the right scale to instantly become something else without much work. A bedhead, for example, like one of my all time favorites, Beatrice, the Fairytale padded bedhead (p. 58). And, of course, the smallest picture frames are a natural just as they are. Paint a group of them a single color for some easy miniverse decorating.

The Stretcher
Long thin frames instantly attract my attention. Use them for Berit platform bed (p. 66), a shower screen (p. 72), and so on.

The Flatfront
This is a frame made in a flat solid piece, usually wood, with a hole cut for the picture. These make easy wall units with a bit of dressing up. Eden wall unit is made from a flatfront, just perfect for Edura TV (p. 34).

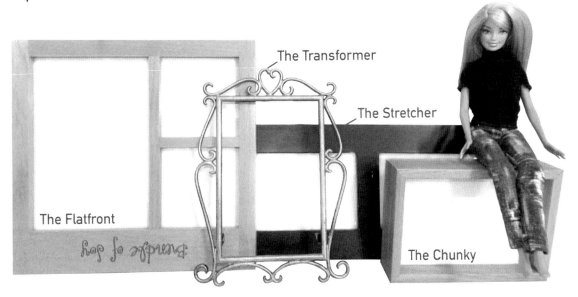

The Transformer

The Stretcher

The Flatfront

The Chunky

02 Toppers

Toppers are anything that will make a table top. It must be firm, smooth on one side and unbreakable. Acrylic, wood, coasters, box lids, plaques and backings from picture frames all work well.

03 Candle Sticks, Candle Holders, and Oil Burners

These little beauties have all the right qualifications. Strong materials, often metal, and lots of pretty bling designed to get them bought in the first place. These are fashionable items like photo frames, that end up undamaged but discarded for the next eye catching beauty.

Now, which one to take home?
Look carefully at the design. Is it dainty enough to look good at 1:6 scale? If it could become a table or stool, make sure it stands square so a topper put on top will sit parallel to the floor.

The plastic trims can be prised off and the back of the plaque makes a perfect table top with "carved" edges

04 Packaging

Where to start? With lids, of course. And nozzles, food containers, and boxes.

I keep them all. From the most boring soft drink bottle screw top to the designer stoppers for perfume bottles, any lid can have an alternative life at 1:6 scale

Cosmetic packaging is made to catch the eye. And often the tops are made from clear acrylic or metallic material that is perfect as it is. No work involved. I love that!

Look out for packaging that is really 1:6 scale furniture in disguise. It could be a shelf unit for example. Or a cupboard. Or even a refrigerator like Katie (p. 39)!

05 Ballpoint Pens

Every piece has potential. Lovely machined parts, all absolutely identical. Perfect for table legs (the barrels), short legs (the pen tops or the screw on bits at the top and bottom), bedhead posts, light fittings, doodads of all kinds, and even miniature makeup from the empty tube that holds the ink. Take them apart and see what you get!

06 Boxes and Bases

Most furniture is a box, more or less. I never throw out a nice box. From cutlery canteens to import miniatures, they are all keepers. And cardboard boxes are fine too. Free! For these projects, they can make a bed, or sofa, for the cost of some glue and some fabric from your stash. The supermarket universe is chockfull of them, all free! Hardware boxes are often sturdier. Solid timber lengths make great bases for sofas, beds and chairs, and can often be scavenged, already cut to suitable lengths, from the waste piles at building sites. I always ask, and have always been given cheerful permission to take as many as I want! Cheap artist's canvases are good too, if you can find suitable sizes.

07 Buttons and Beads

Bright shiny things. I love all jewelry, and all beads. Some are more useful than others.

The world is full of round beads, and how very nice they are too!
But more unusual shapes are precious. When I see flat, oval, hexagonal, and most especially, cube beads, my playscale goggles flash with interest. That's because cubes can be handy reinforcement for our mini glue jobs, just glued into place to add strength.

Buttons are wonderful. Big ones for lamp bases, flat ones for plates, or pretty ones for dressing table minis. Metallic buttons are hard to get and precious for saucepan lids.

I buy most of my buttons, trims and fabrics at local thrift stores. They are a fraction of retail price and best of all, they are often tiny amounts for tiny prices. Just what I need!

08 Dominos

Cheap plastic dominoes have lots of uses. Ordinary craft glue works well with them And they come in little wooden boxes that make sweet shelves.

09 Coasters, and their holders

This is another houseware staple that starts with appealing design, and survives undamaged, ready for a new life with a starring role. Smooth, tough, and just the right size for 1:6 scale.

10 Neckties for cushions and upholstery

Buy only the prettiest. And only what you can use. Both silk and polyester ties can be handwashed. Be warned, they are addictive!

Any ordinary household goodies to keep?
Champagne corks (to cut into suitable chunks to glue things together); transparent sheet packaging; paperclips; tubing from spray bottles; pretty papers, trims and cardboards. Take a good look at whatever you are throwing out. Drawer and door handles. Light fittings. Crayon stubs (for candles) Anything wooden. Tins (no sharp edges!) Metal press lids from powdered products. And so on.

Any wooden item like this salt and pepper shaker goes straight into the stash.

Chapter Two
The Basics

I had better come clean— I hate complicated instructions. I don't measure things much. I don't measure things accurately. No two items that I make are ever exactly alike. Power tools are too noisy, and much too scary.

And yet…it doesn't seem to matter. We love the finished product. And children, especially, don't look for imperfections. A smart choice of color, fabric and trim make for that magic eye appeal. So who cares about precision?

I just want to make fun things. So here are my tips for how to make minis.

01 Cutting Things

I have used my trusty craft knife throughout this book. Why? This book is a power-saw-free zone. Luckily, 3 ply wood cuts very nicely with a craft knife. Any craft knife that you have is fine. Mine is a Stanley Fatmax and I like it because I have finally figured out how to change the blade. Of course, sharper is always better. Google your model if you have forgotten how to change the blade!

To make a neat corner when cutting 3 ply or cardboard, cut straight through from both directions. Sand edges by holding at a right angle to fine sandpaper.

Glues and Paints

I have no idea what is in glues or paints that makes them behave like glues or paints, and furthermore, I really don't want to know. But they are all potentially toxic, so follow the instructions, work in a ventilated space and wash hands especially before eating. And train children to do the same.

My best tip is for before you start, and involves brains rather than technology:

Stop and think! How will you hold your adorable mini to paint it, and how will you leave it to dry? Will it sit on a flat surface? Does it need something to sit on? Some plastic putty might do the job. Would it glue together better with some pressure applied? We can use anything from a proper G-clamp to a paperclip.

02 Painting Things

For this book, I wanted to avoid speciality paints and complicated paint finishes. I have used sample pots of ordinary household acrylic paint from the hardware store. No fancy paints at all! I mix white paint to make paler shades. Craft store paints are fine too. I use cheap artist's brushes from the import store or the smallest hardware store brushes.

We like to paint things that were not meant to be painted, like packaging, so a decent primer is an essential. I use an ordinary interior acrylic primer. Add topcoat of clear varnish or even clear nail polish; it works like a charm. Just be sure to try on a concealed spot first!

03 Gluing Things

So many glues, so little time. We just want things to stick together, preferably right away.

A glue gun is good for quick, large jobs, but makes blobs that are too big for many of our minis.

All purpose craft glue in a bottle is a winner. A bit slow in drying but does lots of our tasks well. Some jobs are small enough to apply with something pointy, like a toothpick, to avoid blobs. Or use some cardboard as a spreader for flat surfaces.

Spray adhesive is great for upholstery, like our sofas. Use a cardboard box with the top and one side cut out for a mini spray booth.

My all time fave, the All Plastics superglue, works beautifully on all kinds of plastics, including recycled domestic products like PET.

We often want to get some extra strength into our glue job, especially to glue things at right angles. A bit of help from some extra material glued into place is a good idea. Square beads can be pushed into corners, or lengths of skewers can run alongside a joint. And chunks of champagne cork cut easily into odd shapes to go just about anywhere they won't be seen. The quick trick to making any of these invisible if you do not want to paint, is to color with a matching felt tip marker for instant camouflage.

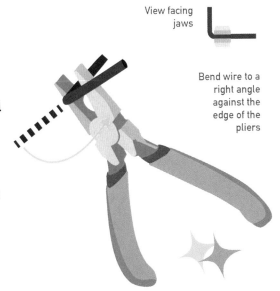

View facing jaws

Bend wire to a right angle against the edge of the pliers

04 Bending and cutting wire

Use a good sturdy pair of large combination pliers and a small pair for finer work. No secrets here!

To cut thick wire like coat hanger wire, place the cutting point of the pliers where the cut is to go and wiggle the waste end gently back and forth until it snaps. The waste end might get a bit bent but the important piece stays straight.

To bend wire, like coat hanger wire, hold it firmly across the jaws of the pliers. Push on it as close as you can to the jaws. This keeps the wire straight.

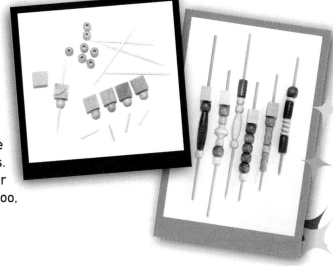

05 Bead legs and Feet

We love detailed, traditional wooden furniture, and we make it with beads, especially for table and chair legs. Choose beads to suit, glue onto skewer or coat hanger wire and don't forget to glue the beads to each other too, for extra strength.

06 Upholstery

Mini upholstery makes stunning dollhouse furniture, and it is so easy! The magic is in working with adorable fabrics to get realistic results without too much work. When gluing foam, be careful not to compress it. The little partitions in the foam stick together and that makes it lumpy. Use a tiny amount of glue, just enough to hold it in place while you cover it. And handle it gently until the glue dries.

It is always a good idea to get rid of excess fabric from inner corners, folds, and seam allowances. If it can't be seen in the finished piece, consider trimming it off!

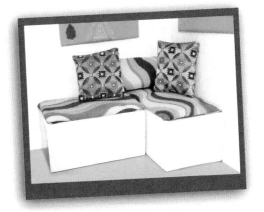

The Upholstered Softie Pad

Card + padding + fabric and glue. This is the easy way to make bespoke upholstery. Cut cardboard to size, and padding exactly the same. Cut the fabric 2-3cm larger all around than the finished piece will be. Cut V shaped notches in the seam allowance for rounded pads, and make diamond corners (see below) or simple folds for a right angled softie pad.

Finish strip

A finish strip is just a piece of fabric with two opposite edges ironed under, made to a particular size. The instructions will say to make a finish strip of a certain size and tell you which sides to iron under. I find that easier than starting with a piece of fabric and struggling to iron tiny folds accurately. This way, you can start with a bigger piece of fabric and trim the waste when you have the right size.

The Diamond Corner

This is the way to get a nice corner on flat items. It takes the extra fabric out of the way to the underside where it can't be seen.

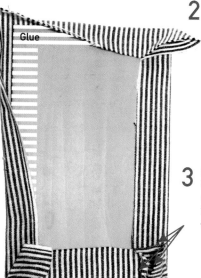

1 Put a thin layer of glue on the piece in the L-shaped corner area.

Glue

2 Glue fabric to a diagonal line from the corner.

3 Put a drop of glue inside the ear, and on the valley on each side. You can trim the waste off the top of the ear if you like.

4 Press the ear flat to make a diamond.

The Square Edge Wrap

This is good for making neat corners. The fabric runs along the corners like real upholstery and doesn't leave angled folds where they can be seen from the sides, the way a parcel wrap does.

1. Choose the sides that will be most visible, like the front of a sofa. Glue the other sides down first. They will end up with folds visible curving around the ends.

2. Pull one free end out into a flap. At the same time push the fabric around the corner, from the glued side.

3. Pull the flap into place along the corner. A little triangular flap will form on the underside. Put glue inside it, under it and on top of it. Press flap into place and glue down. Do the other end exactly the same.

The Wrapperflap

We often want extra fabric to finish a piece neatly, so it looks good from all angles, without unfinished edges. And sometimes for a tidy finish to a project, like Shima sofa (p 28).

The Wrapperflap is just a routine square edge wrap with extra fabric to make a long flap. The extra fabric naturally makes a finish strip to be glued or sewn into place. It is a combination of a Square Wrap and a finish strip! Trim extra fabric from inside the flap.

Now, to get this Wrapperflap into place and I'm done!

Pull fabric around from glued side, pull flap out.

Iron the free edge under to the right size.

01 Sabina Sofa

Sabina Sofa is inspired by Ikea's famous Klippan sofa. Ikea sells gazillions of these babies every year, and has done so since 1979. A true design classic.

I have left the folds a little loose so you can see how they run around the sofa.

The Goodies

- 10 cheap foam dishwashing sponges: They are about 6 x 9cm and 2.5cm deep, but the size can vary a bit. The exact sizing is not crucial for this project, so adjust if necessary.
- Cardboard adds some firmness and weight. It holds the sponges together for the seat and back, so a nice thick piece is good.
- Fabric: Pick a smartie geometric print for that Ikea style. And any little glitches will be hidden.
- Glue: Use mainly a craft glue for the upholstery, to glue down all those little triangles. Aerosol glue is fun for the bigger wrap jobs.

The Babysteps

The sponges assemble into four pieces: the seat, the back and two identical arms. They all get a wrap, then are glued together. See The Basics for the Square Edge and Wrapperflap details (p. 09).

1 Arms: Each arm is a single sponge and gets covered all round with a simple square edge wrap. Cut fabric big enough to cover the whole sponge.

Two small tweaks produce a convincing upholstered look.

The first is to place the short end (the top or bottom of the arms) a bit closer to one end of the fabric than the other before you start the wrap. This puts the line where the flaps meet off centre so it can be hidden by the seat when the sofa is assembled.

The second is to start the wrap along the long edges of the sponge.

Start the wrap for the arms by gluing along the long edges of the sponge first.

10

Below: Sabina Sofa, Sadie Ottoman p. 13
Clockwise from left: Edura T.V. p. 34,
Addison Planter p. 17, Alice Frames p. 52,
Sacha Chair p. 12, Sabina Sofa, Tamara
Coffee Table p. 12

Sponges are glued to cardboard, wrapped, and assembled like this.

Cardboard strengthens the seat and back of the sofa.

Back of Sofa

Bottom of Sofa

2 Seat: Strip the green layer from 4 sponges. They make the seat with cardboard at the bottom and in between.

3 Cut cardboard—2 identical pieces just a little smaller than the seat. Glue the seat in two layers so that cardboard will be at the bottom for a neat finish and soft foam on the top to make the seat. The sequence from the bottom is cardboard, sponge, cardboard, sponge. Wrap the seat. The sides and back will be concealed, so there is no need to fuss over the details.

4 Back: Four sponges make the back Glue to a slightly smaller piece of card. The card faces the back of the sofa, and will be covered by fabric.

5 Cut fabric to completely wrap the backpiece. We want the fabric to meet on the soft side of the backpiece and closer to one long edge than the other. Just like the arms, we want the fabric to meet closer to the bottom of the back piece than to the top. That way the join will be covered by the sofa seat when they are glued together. So to start the wrap, place the sofa back, cardboard side down, on the fabric, and make the start and finish of the wrap off-center. Glue the short edges first.

6 Assemble on a flat surface. For a neat finish, we want to conceal the join in the upholstery so place the back and arms with the fabric join facing inwards where it will be covered by the seat. Glue and done!

11

02 *Sacha* *Armchair*

The Goodies
- 6 dishwashing sponges
- Fabric
- Cardboard
- Glue

The Babysteps

1 The Arms: Made exactly the same as Sabina.

2 The Back: Two sponges side by side, stuck to cardboard cut about 10x7cm. Wrap just like Sabina.

3 The Seat: Strip the green bits off two sponges. The sponges have to be trimmed to fit between the arms. They can vary a bit. I trimmed 2.5cm from these, which made a cube. The sponges can be cut with ordinary household scissors.

4 Steps 4-6: As for Sabina except that the back has 2 sponges instead of 4.

03 *Tamara* Coffee Table

Door handles can often be scrounged for free, when furniture is discarded. It was fashionable a few years ago to use wooden D handles, and they are very good to work with. To make a coffee table, look for U or D shapes. The legs can be made longer using the ready made screw holes at the ends to add beads if you like.

The Goodies
- A coaster for the top
- Suitable handles

The Babysteps

1 Glue! For these handles, I used my All Plastics superglue. Craft glue didn't work!

2 You can strengthen the join by gluing bamboo skewer pieces into the angle where the handle runs underneath the topper.

04 Sadie Ottoman

Fashionable ottomans for a few cents.
Silk, ready-made upholstery.
Indestructible. Ten minutes to make,
and beautiful.

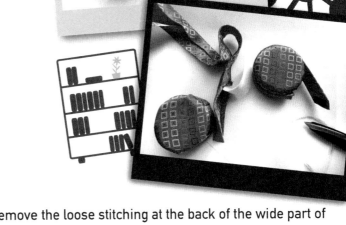

Finished Sadie shown on p. 10.

The Goodies

♥ Pick a lovely tie. Geometrics for a grown up look, patterns, or pretty pastels. Sadie is very adaptable. Pick a full width tie. We use the widest part to cover the seat and the narrow end for the sides.

♥ You also need a tin can 4-5cm high. Tuna cans work well.

♥ Thin foam or any padding.
You can use the padding from inside the tie or foam for a squishier ottoman.

The Babysteps

1 Cut a circle of foam the size of the can. Just draw around the can to get the size. Glue foam to the top of the can.

2 Remove the loose stitching at the back of the wide part of the tie and open it out. Cut a circle 3cm larger all around than the can from the fabric.

3 Cover the top of the seat with the fabric circle from Step 2.

4 Glue the narrow end of the tie around the sides, finishing with the V shaped end for a neat finish. Instant upholstery!

05 Tessa Dining Table

The Goodies

♥ Shallow lid with a rim
♥ Nozzles from syringe style cannisters like adhesive caulk that builders and plumbers use
♥ White adhesive paper

The Babysteps

1 Color the nozzles with felt pen if you like.

2 Glue to underside of table. Make sure that you glue to the inside of the rim to get more strength to the bond.

3 Add white adhesive paper sheet to fit top of table and a narrow strip for the edge.

06 *Sally* Dining Chair

Coat hangers, tape, padding, and fabric. Sally has a slim modern shape and the quick upholstery makes everything look very professional. Sally can be made for a few cents and some scraps, and she is a real eye catcher in a special fabric like faux leather.

The Goodies

- One coat hanger per chair. Pick the thicker kind if you can, and a nice shiny finish is good
- Tape: 50mm tape is easiest but thinner will do the job
- Fabric: Not too thin, pick a fabric with some firmness but which makes crisp folds.

  The long lower strip of the hanger and the curved ends make one chair.

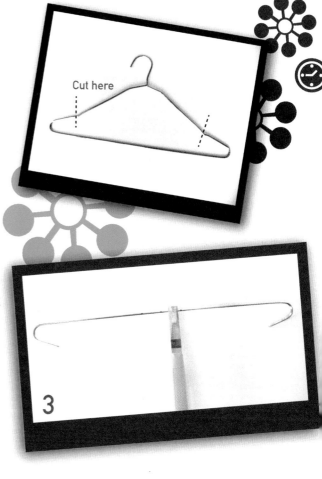

Cut here

The Babysteps

1 Cut hanger 30-40mm from the ends (See photo). The short ends make the seat back, so the longer you cut them, the higher the back will be.

2 Measure the wire and mark it at the middle. This is one time to be as accurate as you can, so the curves from seat to back will line up after the wire is bent into shape. But don't worry too much, the upholstery conceals lots!

3

Now we are going to make the corners of the seat frame. There are only six to make the chair, so take your time. Try to use the same method for each or the six bends. The rule is "Hold the Middle, Bend the Ends". Use sturdy pliers to grasp the wire. You can protect the wire finish with a strip of cardboard if you like. Place pliers at right angles to the planned corner and just inside the mark by about 3mm to allow for the curve of the wire. Bend the wire around the pliers with even pressure close to the corner rather than at the end of the wire. This keeps the wire straight.

3 Back lower corners: Mark 3cm either side of the midpoint. Hold wire just inside the 3cm mark, with pliers in the same line as the cut hooks of wire. Bring the end forward to a right angle. Do the same on the other side. We now have a U shape with hooks on each end. Take time to get the U shape to sit flat. This is the bottom of the chair.

4 Mark out the sides, front legs, and seat sides. Measure from the rear corner we just made, to the point the wire starts to curve. Divide into three. The measurements don't have to be precise, but try to get the sides the to match, more or less.

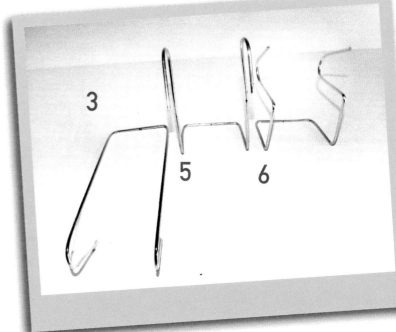

Postcards make fun artwork! This one is by Ikea's Eva Lundgren.

Clockwise from left:
Annabelle Plants p. 67, Sally Chair, Tessa Table p. 13,
Madhu Candles p. 26, Madonna Plates p. 40, Maggie Food p. 40,
Abby Blinds p. 16, Ada Scrolls p. 17, Addison Planter p. 17.

To help the doll sit better in the chair, make the seat dip slightly towards the back.

5 Front corners: Start with the hooked ends facing downward (see photo) and bend upwards to form the lower front corner.

6 Bend back to make the top front corners. Each side is 3 sides of a square attached to the back crosspiece. Straighten the curved cut ends to make the back.

7 Tape makes the support for the upholstery. Cut strips to run across the back and seat around the wire. Start 1 cm back from the front corner so the tape does not get in the way of the upholstery later. Then run tape twice, top to bottom around the seat and back. Repeat until it all feels quite firm.

8 For the upholstery, make a finish strip 5mm wider than the chair with the long edges ironed under. It should be longer than needed to wrap the chair front and back, with an extra 3mm for closure at the front. Iron under one short end.

9 The finished short end runs across the front of the chair. Fix it in place with a small piece of tape while you work. Flip the strip over the back (a). Sew along both sides, placing the front over the back for a realistic finish. Then sew closed across the front (b).

9a

9b

15

07 *Abby* *Bamboo Blind*

So many gorgeous mini blinds are disguised as bamboo placemats! Natural, colored, thick slats, thin slats. They are very cheap to buy new and easy to find second hand, often unused. With a few tricks, they make adorable, speedy window treatments with a surprise "Wow!" appeal.

The Goodies
- Bamboo placemats made of cut bamboo
- Skewers, or lengths of coat hanger wire (Optional)

The Babysteps

Before you start! These placemats are held together by rows of stitching and will fall apart before your eyes once it is cut! So read through the instructions before you cut.

1 This mat has a firm slat to make a heading and is just glued into place. You can make a roller at top or bottom by rolling and gluing the mat. To hang the mat on screw hooks, wrap around skewer or coat hanger wire that is a bit longer than the roll. And the roll has to fit between the hook and the window frame, so it can't be too big.

2 Now we are ready to cut the original stitching. But not right at our new edge. Oh, no, no, no. Cut at least 5 slats below that. We need enough loose string to knot. The extra slats pull out to leave little tails of string. Knot them if you can, or just twist them with a little dab of glue and stick them to the back of the blind.

3 Glue to wall or frame.

Blind too wide? Snip the bamboo slats with pliers. Or tin snips if you have them. But before you start, check where the rows of stitching will run on the finished blind. It will hang better if the stitching is close to the edges. Rule a line where you want to cut. Hold the blind firmly to cut a neat line. Plan to have the machine cut end facing the front of the mini room where it will be most visible.

08 *Ada* *Scroll Artwork*

The Goodies

- Scrap of fabric with an interesting image
- Skewer or coat hanger wire
- Thick thread (embroidery thread)
- Beads

The Babysteps

1 Select image and cut out with 1.5cm extra on edges.

2 Turn under fabric along the sides and glue or hand sew into place

3 Cut rod just a little longer than the width of the scroll and roll the top of the fabric around it, gluing as you go.

Optional extra: Do the same to the bottom. It will hang better with both ends rolled.

4 Tie thread to make a hanger. Add beads to ends of the hanger. A push pin makes an easy wall fitting to hang your scroll.

09 *Addison* *Planter*

These candleholders are so realistic as planters. I had to have them! But they have the candle still inside! Difficult to remove, so don't even try. Use the candle to make a really quick but adorable mini. Little kids love doing this and think that you are an incredibly clever grown up. You can make a splendid flower arrangement like this too!

The Goodies

- Candle holder with candle
- Aquarium or Bonsai gravel
- Artificial foliage

The Babysteps

1 Light the candle and let it burn until there is a big soft area in the middle. Spread the wax around the top and press gravel into it. Make a hole with a sharp point in the middle and push the plant in.

2 Let it cool. Tip out any loose gravel. Mix more gravel with some clear nail polish (mix it on top of something you can throw away, like packaging) and add to the top, with lots more nail polish to hold it all together.

10 Samantha *Sofa*

Samantha has two easy upholstered parts: the seat and the backpiece. The backpiece is made from cardboard and curves gracefully around the oval seat. Very nice. The bespoke upholstery is a simple envelope pulled over the padded cardboard and glued or handstitched closed. Nothing is difficult and it all gets done with surprising speed.

The Goodies

- A curved tin: This tin is 210cm long but adapt to what you have.
- Pen bits or beads for the feet
- Cardboard: If you would like Samantha to have true heirloom potential, use a sturdy cardboard. Cereal box card won't last.
- Fabric
- Thin foam
- Glue

This tin is 210 cm long and the measurements are for that size.
The fabric is best cut on the bias for the front of the backpiece, which means that patterns will run crossways, so chose an all over pattern like this floral one.

And Samantha is adaptable. Anything from bright and cheery to dressed-up formal. Just choose your fabric.

The Babysteps

1. Make the seat. If the tin has no lid, fill the tin with corrugated cardboard cut to size. Place a layer of foam padding on top.

2. Cut fabric to cover the outside of the tin and turn underneath, using the tin as a guide.

3. Glue fabric over seat and sides, making small pleats to fit. Add glue to anything you don't like and flatten it out.

4. Glue legs to bottom. Bead feet look good. I made these just like bead legs. Or use pen bit feet. (see The Basics p. 08)

5. Pull fabric firmly to underside and glue, pleating as necessary and trimming around feet.

18

9 Cut fabric cover. This is the backpiece with a seam allowance of 1.5cm all around and 3cm on the bottom. Cut two: one the bias and one on the straight grain.

10 Sew cover. Place right sides together and sew with a small stitch around the curves, leaving the straight side, the bottom, open. Cut V notches into the allowance and turn cover right side out.

11 Pull cover over the padded backpiece with the bias fabric to the inside of the backpiece. Stitch or glue closed.

6 Make a pattern for the backpiece. Use a circular object like a large cup to get the curves. It should be about half the circumference of the tin. In this case, it was 29cm long. Adapt as you like but keep the shape smooth so the cover will sit well.

To get the pattern exactly the same both sides, fold at the middle and cut both sides of the pattern together.
See sample half pattern in the background of this page (pink shading).

7 Cut backpiece from sturdy cardboard.

8 Cut thin padding 3cm bigger all around and glue to front of card. Cut V shapes into the turnover edges so it will sit flat, fold extra padding to the back and glue.

12 Glue backpiece into place around the seat and hold in place overnight with rubber bands. Done!

11 Savannah
Armchair

The Babysteps

Savannah is made exactly the same as Samantha. Use an oval tin 6-10cm long. Beware of sardine cans: they often angle towards the base. It can look good but might not be a match for your beautiful version of Samantha. This one contained sweets.

Modify the cardboard backpiece using our pattern or something like a drinking glass to make the curves.

12 Tina Coffee Table

I wanted a delicate table with really elegant legs. Tough to manage at 1:6 scale without serious woodwork? Well, yes. So what we use is a lid with a rim, to have a good surface for our glue job, bead legs (see The Basics p. 08), some glue, and some cunning.

The Goodies

- ♥ Lid with a rim, sized for a small table ie 6-10cm. This one is metal. Plastic is fine too.
- ♥ Coat hanger wire or skewers. Skewers make for a really easy job, although not quite as rigid as wire, but if you don't much like tools, use fine skewers to fit your beads and cut with scissors.
- ♥ Beads
- ♥ Glue: A glue gun works fine for this.
- ♥ Paint

The Babysteps

1 Make 4 identical bead legs. I fancied a faux bamboo look for these. The top bead must have a flat surface to glue to the underside of the lid. For a strong glue bond, choose one that will nestle inside that irritating little curled rim on the edge of the tin. Glue the beads to each other end to end, as well as onto the supporting skewer or wire.

2 Glue to underside of lid

3 Paint, and Done!

This tin does double duty! I used the lid for Tina, and the tin for Savannah!

20

13 *Titania* Pedestal Table

The Goodies

- Plastic lids and nozzles
- Coaster or lid for a topper
- Coat hanger wire or skewer
- Rounds of cork e.g. from champagne corks
- Glue, paint

The Babysteps

1 Drill or hot wire holes through the centers of the lids

2 Play with the order of lids and nozzles until you like the effect.

3 Place rounds of cork inside each and push skewer or wire. through to assemble, gluing as you go.

14 *Tomasina* Dining Table

Our princess will require somewhere to entertain, somewhere to count her tiaras and so on. Tomasina is a glue and paint job. A small picture frame makes the underskirt. What a fun way to add strength to the join and some "carving" too!

The Goodies

- Plywood, or any suitable topper
- 2 craftwood letters "H" about 9cm tall, "X" will also work, or "M", depending on how it's cut.
- Small square or rectangular picture frame or cut piece of plywood

The Babysteps

1 Cut the plywood top. This one is 13 x 11cm.

2 Glue the picture frame centered on the underside of the tabletop.

3 Glue the letters to both the underside of the table and the edge of the picture frame/underskirt.

4 Paint and done!

15 *Sharmila* Dining Chair

Clockwise from left: Sharmila Chair. Tomasina Table p. 21. Annabelle Plants p. 67

Very crafty project this one. The chair is lovely, but this is probably the fussiest project in the book. Plan to work in stages over a day and take your time. The results are worth it. A classic chair with no woodwork, love it!

The Goodies

- ♥ Beads
- ♥ Skewers or coat hanger wire
- ♥ Cardboard boxes about 6cm x 6cm (e.g. cracker boxes)
- ♥ Corrugated cardboard)
- ♥ Fabric

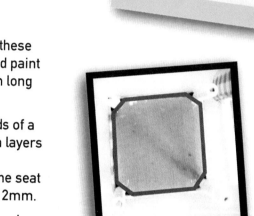

The Babysteps

1 The legs are bead legs (See The Basics p. 08). I made these to match Tina table (p 20). Just a suggestion: make and paint the bead legs ahead of time. They should be about 6cm long and they fit into the corners of the box.

2 The seat is made from a shallow box, cut from the ends of a cracker box or any other suitable small box, filled with layers of cardboard pasted together to make a firm seat. Cut squares of corrugated cardboard to fit the box. Make the seat deep enough for at least 3 layers of cardboard, about 12mm.

3 Trim all the corners of the cardboard squares so the beads legs will fit firmly. Make triangles for round legs like these (See photo).

3 For round legs, snip ends of cardboard square to make a triangle shaped hole.

4 Cover the edges of the seat. Use a small finish strip (see The Basics p. 08) the depth of the seat, ironed along the long ends and long enough to wrap all around ie about 24cm if you started with a 6cm square seat.) Start and finish will be hidden once the seat is assembled. Glue into place. You can use a ribbon for this if you want a contrasting color. Bring the lower end of the finish strip under the edge of the box for a neat edge.

5 Glue layers of cardboard together and then into the box. Use lots of glue.

6 Glue the legs into their little triangular niches with a very generous amount of glue because it will tend to disappear into the cardboard.

7 Cut strips of cardboard the width of the seat and 24cm long, with the ribs of the cardboard running along the short side so it will bend easily to make the seat and back of the chair.

8 Now to make the rest of the chair. Hold the cardboard strip lined up against the bottom of the seat at both front and back. Starting at the front, gently shape the corrugated card to fit over the seat Make a sharp fold at the back of the seat and bring the cardboard to a right angle, and another sharp fold at the top to make the double layer for the seat back (See photo).

9 Cover one side of the strips with fabric, with a turnunder to the other side. This will be hidden inside the double fold of the back.

10 Glue strip into place. It should fit neatly.

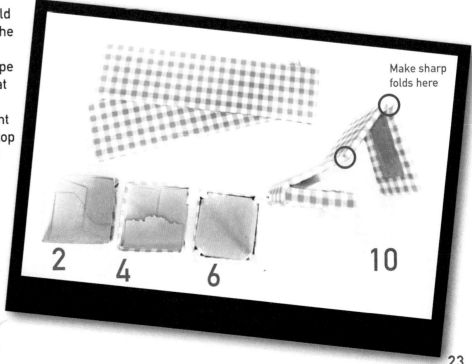

Make sharp folds here

2 4 6 10

16 Macey Cake

A fun mini for a special birthday!

The Goodies

- White plastic lids of different sizes
- Skewer or wire
- Cork
- Colored Paperclips
- White four-hole button
- Thin Ribbon

A small metal press lid turned upside down makes a cake stand.

The Babysteps

1 Make a hole through the center of all the lids except for the smallest lid.

2 Glue pieces of cork into the centre of each lid. Push skewer or wire through lids from largest to smallest, adding plenty of glue as you go.

3 Glue narrow ribbon to the bottom of each tier of your cake.

4 Glue button to the top of the cake and push short bits of colored paperclip into the holes for candles.

5 Varnish with clear nail polish (optional).

17 Ebba *Skirted Table*

The Goodies

- ♥ Shallow lid or box, any shape
- ♥ Fabric
- ♥ Ribbon, braid or bias binding
- ♥ Bow or other decorative detail
- ♥ Support for the table like a block of wood

The Babysteps

1 Cover the top and sides of the lid, using a square edge wrap (See The Basics p. 09).

2 Cut a strip of fabric 6cm longer than needed to go around the table. Hem one long end and one short end. Make it just shorter than the drop from the middle of the table edge to the bottom of the support.

3 Glue table top to support. Glue skirt to edge of tabletop, starting from the back, with the hemmed edge to the bottom. Make tiny pleats at the top as you glue. Put a tiny dab of glue inside and under the fold and press down. Make them really small, because we don't want too much bulk in the skirt.

4 Cover the raw edge with trim and add bow or decoration. Done!

18 Topaz *Table*

This is a good project to do with a young child, because it's quick. Glue, paint, and done!

The Goodies

- ♥ Metal press lid or any suitable topper. A coaster is a good size, too.
- ♥ Length of manufactured beading to fit inside the rim of the lid.
- ♥ Interesting bits and pieces to stack for the pedestal (blocks of wood, salt shakers, eggcups, large beads, pieces of plywood, and so on.)

The Babysteps

1 Glue the beading into the rim of the lid. What an elegant edging! Spread a thin layer of glue inside that little rim with a skewer and be sure to wipe away any excess glue.

2 Glue the pedestal together, and add the topper. Add trims like an alphabet charm or "carving" to the pedestal (optional).

3 Paint, and done!

19 *Madhu* Candles

The Goodies
- ♥ Beads
- ♥ Flat head drawing pins
- ♥ Birthday candles
- ♥ Crayons
- ♥ Skewers
- ♥ Q tips
- ♥ Long thin beads

My favorite thin candle is the flat end of a skewer. Very hardy and looks good. Crayons are not suitable for rough play.

The Babysteps
Cut the candles to length by gently turning under the blade of a craft knife. For candle holders for large candles like crayons, look for beads with large holes or be prepared to drill. For flat jewelry findings or beads, poke a flat head drawing pin through the hole and push the candle onto it, otherwise glue together.

These are tiny and have a natural tendency to be eaten by vacuum cleaners. Think about glueing several into a bigger display on a tray or something flat, like a domino.

20 *Aditi* Reading Lamp

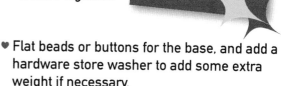

The Goodies
- ♥ Suitable bead, pen bit (the conical bit that holds the writing tip in place), packaging cap like bottle top from eyedrops.
- ♥ Any firm wire like coat hanger wire, coated or uncoated, or softer wires twisted together.
- ♥ Flat beads or buttons for the base, and add a hardware store washer to add some extra weight if necessary.

The Babysteps

1 The wire has to connect well to the base, so drill a hole to match the wire. Or use a suitable bead on top of the base as a connector.

2 Then, just glue! Play with the curve of the wire so the lamp stands well. A lightweight shade, like the trumpet shaped bead, is easier.

21 Admina Roller Blinds

Admina looks very realistic for very little work. This "roller" version doesn't open, and needs a only a small amount of fabric.

The Goodies

♥ Fabric
♥ Skewer or firm wire
♥ Narrow ribbon, braid or lace for trim
♥ Beads for finials.

Admina is a rectangle of fabric with all four sides turned under. A deeper hem at the top makes the fabric roll.

The Babysteps

1 Cut fabric 3cm wider and 6cm longer than the finished blind.

2 Turn under the sides and bottom of the blind 1.5cm and sew or glue. Do the sides first for a neater finish along the bottom edge of the blind. Make the top turnunder 3cm deep.

3 Add a trim if you like. Cut trim long enough to glue around the to back of blind. Put a weight on the flat part of the blind to keep it flat as the glue dries.

4 The blind roller is made by rolling the top of the blind towards the front around a length of skewer or wire, gluing as you go. Make the skewer/wire long enough to sit on screw hooks with beads for finials, or hide it inside the roll and simply glue the blind into the frame.

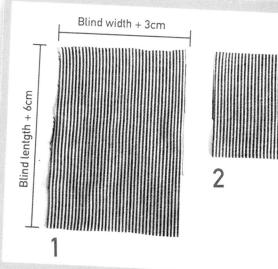

Blind width + 3cm

Blind lentgth + 6cm

1 2 4

4

Cover the backpiece

Start with the lower back corners

bottom of sofa

Extra long flap will go over seat back

22 Shima Sofa

Shima is an easy wrap job.
What a clever girl!

The Goodies

- ♥ Sofa sized piece of timber or box
- ♥ Fabric to cover
- ♥ Thick cardboard or thin plywood for the back, at least 5cm shorter than the sofa base
- ♥ Thin foam or padding
- ♥ Glue, tape (optional)

The Babysteps

1 Upholster the back. The upholstery for the sofa back is very easy because the lower part will be covered when the seat is wrapped. Glue foam to top 2/3 of one side. This is now the front. Cover the top 2/3 front and back (see the picture). If your fabric has a design like this one, make sure it is running the right way.

2 Cut and glue foam to cover one big and one small side of the seat block, for the front and seat of the sofa.

3 Cut fabric to cover the seat component. It will wrap the whole block with extra to cover the join to the backpiece. It should be wide enough to go across the length of the seat, down both sides and under the bottom of the sofa. It has to be long enough to go right around the seat front to back, plus 12cm extra. Any extra gets trimmed off at the end so this is not a precise measurement.

4 Square edge wrap the rear corners (the corners without any foam) with a small turnunder to the bottom of the sofa. Very routine. Then square edge wrap the front corners. The rest of the fabric will make an extra long wrapper flap. Glue it to the bottom of the sofa. Stop there.

5 Now put the back into place, padding to the front. Center it and make sure it is level from the front. Glue the two pieces together and run tape over the join at the lower back if you like. This is not necessary, just adds a bit of extra strength.

6 Bring the fabric upwards around the back corner and over the sofa back to cover the join to the seat. Trim fabric as required. Turn long end under and glue down for a neat finish. Add buttons or flat beads for feet if you like.

23 *Sonomi*
Ottoman

Sonomi s a 10 minute mini, especially if you already have all the goodies ready to make Shima.

The Goodies
- Block of wood
- Foam
- Fabric

The Babysteps

1 Cover the top of the block with foam.

2 Cut fabric to make a square edge wrap and finish underneath. Square edge wrap. Done.

24 Tori Table

Some 1:6 furniture is just too easy!

The Goodies

♥ Tori is what I call a transformer. Take a coaster holder and turn it upside down and…Voila! A perfect little table. As I explained in The Goodies, scavenging is defined as DIY for this book. So put on your 1:6 goggles and go hunting. The little black one even makes a bench. Cute!

25 Sumi Banquette

The Goodies

♥ Box: The box should be about 6cm deep to make the seat. The length can be whatever you fancy. And, yes, the packaging from the World's Most Famous Mobile Phone is perfect for Sumi. Make two for an L-shaped dining alcove. Very 60's.
♥ Cardboard
♥ Padding
♥ Fabric, Glue

The Babysteps

1 Cut card and padding the same size as the box bottom, in this case 110 x 66mm

2 Make an upholstered pad (See Chapter 2 The Basics p. 08). Stick pad to top of box with glue.

26 Akiko Lamp

The Goodies

- Nozzle from squeeze pack like mustard or ketchup
- Skewers
- Plastic lid with a flat top (e.g. deodorant bottle top)
- Cork pieces (optional)

The Babysteps

1 Demo time! The nozzles come apart with some force. I use my small pliers and pry the cones apart. The outer cone always ends up shooting across the room! The other option is to acquire two identical nozzles.

2 Make the base. Some nozzles fit together beautifully-the inner cone is narrow and the outer nozzle sits over it. Some need to be held together. Push pieces of skewer about 6cm long through both and wedge toothpicks as well if needed, adding some glue to the mix as you go.

3 Add your shade. To strengthen the join, you can glue pieces of cork to the inside of the nozzle and the underside of the shade.

Clockwise from left:
Suri Stool, Ebony Bookshelf, Alannah
Artwork, Bayo Box Bed p. 56, Baba
Pillows p. 44, Babette Bedding p. 45

27 Ebony
Bookshelf

The Goodies
- Chunky picture frame
- Plywood
- Glue

The Basics
No carpentry here. The frame is a chunky–chunkies are one of my favourite scavenge finds, because, of course, they are playscale furniture in disguise. Ikea makes nice chunkies, and they are easy to find second hand.

1 Plywood shelves we cut as usual with our craft knife. Each shelf is the inside width and depth of the frame. Try to make a tight fit. Then just glue the shelf into the frame.

2 Add shelf supports with lengths of skewer or cube beads for added strength

3 Paint, and done!

28 *Alannah*
Artwork

Inspect your stash. This is a search mission for cute motifs to turn into glam artworks. They make a quick mini, and it is fun to do with a child because it can go straight into the dollhouse.

Patchwork fabrics are lovely and have a good texture for this mini. You can make a big abstract design with this too. Very chic, with serious decorating impact. You can also cut plywood or cardboard to size, or use the backing from a picture frame, to make Alannah.

The Goodies
- Cardboard, plywood, or tiny canvases from the import store. They cost about 50 cents each and make the job very easy indeed.
- Fabric with usable design.
- Spray glue is good for this.

The Babysteps

1 Plan your design for maximum artistic effect.

2 Spread a very thin layer of glue over the front of the canvas. Center the image, and pull the fabric slightly to get rid of bubbles. Trim triangles from the corners. Then turn over and glue the back securely. Or make diamond corners.

3 Attach to walls with glue or hook and loop adhesive dots– or multiple small dabs of plastic putty will keep a light item like this in place surprisingly well. The secret is to use lots of small blobs.

29 *Suri*
Stool

The Goodies
- Small chunky photo frame
- Four pen tops from ball point pens
- Cardboard
- Padding
- Fabric

The Babysteps

1 Trim the pointy bit of the pen top as required.

2 Glue pen tops into the corners of the frame. Use plenty of glue, and include the pointy bit for strength. Paint.

3 Make an upholstered pad (see The Basics p. 08) to fit the top of the stool. This one is 7 x 6cm. Glue to top of stool.

4 (Optional) Coat the paint job, or at least the legs, with clear nail polish when it has dried, for some extra shine and protection.

30 Eden *Wall Shelf*

The Goodies

You know those little studs that go into holes down the insides of cupboards? The ones that fall out and get lost? Well, they are really cheap, and easy to use, because they only need a hole drilled. These come from the import shop, cost $2 for a pack of 18, and are ideal for the dollhouse decorator. After all, they are meant for full scale storage. Lots of elegant 1:6 scale furniture can be designed with these babies.

♥ Picture frame; I bought two identical frames for a few peanuts. Pick a frame with a cute opening that you can decorate as you like. Perhaps Edura Television, or a mirror? A fireplace, maybe?
♥ Cabinetry support studs.

The Babysteps

1 Decide on décor and the place for the shelf.

2 Cut shelf from plywood using your craft knife, and round the corners if you like, by rubbing against some sandpaper. Mine is 9 x 3.5cm.

3 Draw a line for the holes. The shelf will sit just above the line.

4 Drill holes. These supports always seem to need 5mm holes. I start with a small hole, to get it accurately placed on my line, then drill the 5 mm hole. It only takes a minute longer to do it this way, but I do want my shelf to sit straight.

5 Glue supports into place with tiny amount of glue (try not to get glue on the top because the shelf sits here, and we want it to be level) Then add the shelf with a small amount of glue on the back edge and on top of the supports.

6 Paint, including the backing piece. Done.

31 *Edura* Television

Edura is quick to make because nothing has to be cut very accurately.

The Goodies

- Plywood or firm cardboard
- Adhesive paper or tape
- Picture
- Bling for "switches"

The Babysteps

1 Cut plywood or card to size. TVs come in lots of sizes, so pick whatever you want! I made this white TV to fit into Eden wall unit.

2 Glue image into place. If you can, use a pic that goes over the whole surface, so it is very smooth.

3 Start with a strip of tape or adhesive paper about 4cm wide. Cut it into 4 pieces–two that are 2cm shorter than the long edges (the top and bottom), and 2 pieces 3cm longer than the short edges (the sides).

4 The top and bottom strips go on first. Place them in the middle so that there is a bare spot at either end. Then wrap to the back. Remember to put the factory made edging of your adhesive material where it will show! These are placed 5mm in from the top and bottom edges.

5 The side strips wrap to the back with a square cut out at the corners for a neat finish.

6 Cover the back with a rectangle of your tape or adhesive paper.

7 Knobs: Add a stick-on crystal or tiny squares of your adhesive paper. Or maybe none at all. Televisions are very streamlined.

8 Stand: Glue to a flat object like a button or domino. Glue a support like a square bead at the back for strength. The stand for the white model is made from two adhesive skid protectors sandwiched together. One gets cut in half with a small strip removed across the middle, to make a slot for the TV to sit in. They are very sticky so the TV will stay in place quite well. If you want to be able to take the TV out of the stand, put a piece of paper where the bottom of the TV will run before you put the top sections in place.

About the Kitchen

All dollhouses should have a kitchen, of course. But they are tricky to make. No need to have every part of a real kitchen. Pick your favourite elements and leave it at that!

Appliances, doors and drawers are all made the same way. Cardboard is scored and folded on itself to make a neat flat parcel, then decorated. I like to fold rather than cut because it makes it makes a neater edge with good depth to it.

Start by cutting cardboard 2cm larger all around than the finished piece. Score the exact size of the object, trim corners at 45 degrees, fold and glue flaps down.

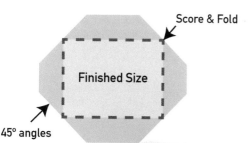

Then cover with photos or paper, folding them around the edges and trimming corners to suit.

Add trims. Push map pins straight through into a piece of cork for sturdy knobs. Lengths of coat hanger wire make trendy long handles. Beads can be glued into place or attached more securely by adding a length of toothpick or skewer pushed through the cardboard.

Use glue or double sided tape to attach the decorated project to cabinets, making sure that the edges are firmly held in place for a "built-in" look.♥

32 Kadira Cabinets

Scrounge and scavenge! Suitable boxes are 10-13cm high for bench height or up to 30 cm for head height.

At 1:6 scale, the counter would be about 10cm deep, which takes up a lot of space. Smaller looks absolutely fine. Mine is only half that depth, made from the lid from a shoe box.

It is easiest to choose cardboard for the sink cabinet to make an easy job of the cutouts for the sink and tap.

A small box with a hinged lid makes a cupboard with an opening door, just for fun.

Everything can be painted, and choose a peppy colour to unify the lot. Of course, painted cardboard will not hold up so well. So if this project is for young children, consider adhesive paper instead, or cover the paint job with clear adhesive paper or spray gloss.♥

33 Kadisha Countertop & Splashback

The countertop and splashback are made in one piece from cardboard wrapped with adhesive paper to imitate laminate. The countertop can be cut just a little larger than the cabinet top at front and sides to look realistic.

And add a splashback to the height you want. Mine is 4cm. Score cardboard lengthways where it will bend at the back of the cabinet. Bend the cardboard to a right angle before you cover with the adhesive paper to avoid wrinkles.

Planning to add a sink to your countertop? Make the cutout now. See Kasey sink (p. 38).

Attach to cabinet top first with double sided tape or glue, then attach to wall.♥

34 Karena
Dishwasher

Make a rectangle to size with scored and folded edge (see diagram on opposite page). This one is 10x7cm finished size.

Wrap with any shiny white paper, or adhesive paper. Add a strip of silver card or paper at the top.

Push a flat top pin though the cardboard for the large control knob and a few small sticky crystals for the indicator lights.♥

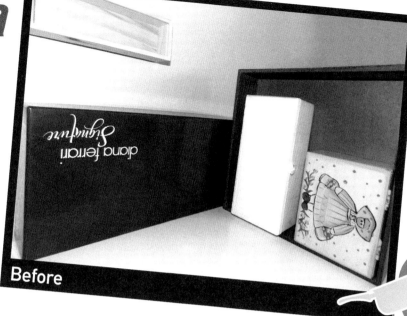

Before

35 Karli
Oven

Use a picture of a real oven on a base of cardboard. Companies make beautiful catalogues to advertise their products. I kept this one from our real life kitchen upgrade. Or you can find a front view of the appliance in an advertising flyer.

Remember to cut extra paper all around to turn under the cardboard base. Cover with clear adhesive paper for a shiny surface or coat with clear nail polish.
Try it on a scrap first! ♥

36 Karolina
Cooktop

Use silver, white or black card for a realistic look, or any color you like for fun. Ready made adhesive circles make the hotplates and circles of white paper cut with an office holepunch make the controls. Add crystals on top for knobs, or push map pins through.♥

Kadira

Karolina

Kadisha

Kadira

Kadira

Karena

Katerina

Kasey

Kat

Katie

37 *Kasey* Sink

Any small container with a lip can be a sink, but this counter is quite small, so a scavenged serving pack is ideal. Look carefully at the packaging next time you are eating airline food!

Cut identical holes though both the cabinet and the countertop. Trace the outside of the lip and cut carefully inside it.

Don't try to rush! Cheap cardboard like shoe boxes tears easily. Just be patient and cut carefully. Slip the sink into place and glue.♥

38 Kat
Taps

Pump packs make good taps. Take one apart and see what you get! Make a hole in the countertop, push the tap through and screw the cap from the original setup back on from the underside. ♥

Screw onto underside

39 Katerina
Exhaust Hood

The thin flip top from a shampoo container is glued to the underside of something long, like a wooden pencil case, timber offcut, or a toothpaste box, painted or covered in white adhesive paper. The lid can be simply attached to the underside of a shelf, too. ♥

40 Katie
Refrigerator

Scavenge! Stationary purchases should be made with a sharp eye for the packaging. The door is the most important and it looks very convincing painted on the inside.

The cute containers on the top shelf are pencil erasers! Also shown: Maegan Milk Carton p. 40, Maisie Plasticware p. 41

Paint the inside including top and bottom of the shelves. The lines of the shelves will show on the outside so paint or cover with white adhesive paper. Both look good, but adhesive paper will wear better.

The fastener on this kind of packaging can be too firm, so a little surgery with a craft knife might be required. Widen the 'claw' that secures the door and or cut off the knob the claw snaps on to.

Glue on a length of coat hanger wire for a handle, and a brand label if you like. ♥

43 Maggie
Food

Small round objects like beads and beans can be a hazard if inhaled by very young children. So this is a project for older children and only if supervised. Use plenty of glue and make sure that the beans are securely fixed to the plate. Add as many thick coats of nail polish as you like.

The goodies for this project mostly came from dry soup mix! The mix that comes straight off the shelf.

Use navy or white beans for potatoes, lentils for meat, green split peas for little mounds of vegetables. Mustard seeds for the pasta or fries. Add a splotch of red nail polish for ketchup.

Place little mounds of glue and press food into place. Coat with clear nail polish for shine. ♥

41 Madonna Plates

Scavenge! Poker chips cost about a buck for twenty and make sweet plates, already decorated with little card designs around the rim.

Otherwise, hoard large flat buttons, especially buttons with a bowl shape. Add a circle of cut out plastic or shiny paper to the middle to cover the holes, or add food! ♥

42 Maegan
Carton

Pick a paper that has a slightly shiny surface, and horizontal blue stripes to look realistic. Or use a citrus image.

The base is about 3cm high and 1cm square. Glue beads to make it.

Cut paper 3cm longer than the base to make the angled top. Overlap the paper along one long edge. Glue to base and along the long edges.

Pinch the free end of the paper wrap into sharp corners, extending up from the base. At the top, push two sides inward to get the right shapes and glue the folds together.

Clamp with a paper clip and allow to dry. Trim top. ♥

44 Maisie
Plasticware

Collect transparent and semiopaque lids (often from makeup and toiletries) to make adorable cannisters. Flat buttons make simple modern lids, like Tupperware containers. Or add a heavy "knob" (a button complete with shank) for a retro look.♥

45 Keisha
Towel Rack

The rack is a shallow U, so make the rack first and then make shallow holes to suit.

Start with about 10cm of coat hanger wire. Hold the middle and bend the ends to get the shape symmetrical.

Make the holes a tight fit. The wood for these cabinets is very soft, so you won't need a drill. Use a sharp point like a small screwdriver. Push into place with a dot of glue. ♥

46 Kelsey
Shelf

Scavenge! Wooden pencil cases and domino boxes from the dollar shop are about the right size, and very inexpensive.

Paint and attach to wall. Add adorable goodies.

Have a look at Eden wall shelf (p. 34) and Barbara wardrobe (p. 50) for some other ideas for shelves. ♥

DOMINO

47 *Mallory* Oven Dish

Find a suitable lid. This is a shampoo bottle lid about 4cm diameter. The handles are made from ordinary hardware rivets, which are very cheap.

Make two holes. Burning with a heated wire is quicker than drilling.

Push rivets through and glue or tape them inside.

Fill with circles of cardboard and use lots of glue. Glue a lid (flat bead or button) to the top. A button with a shank makes a good lid with handle. To use a two hole button, cut a paperclip to make a very long 'U' shape. Modify to fit the holes and push through button. Twist the ends together on the underside. Use a little glue to firm it up and also tape the twisted end to the underside of the lid. ♥

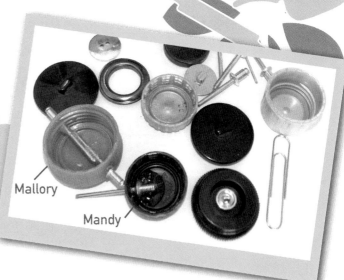

Mallory

Mandy

48 *Mandy* Saucepans & Frying Pans

Drink bottle lids are a good size and come in lovely shiny versions.

Drill or hot wire a hole through the side and push a rivet through to make the handle.

Pack the inside with some cardboard to hold the rivet in place and add some glue. Glue a lid, like the one in Mallory in place. ♥

49 *Maribel* Packaged Food

Start with a box shape that will stand well on its own and is about the right size. I stuck two dominoes together. Cover the tops with colored tape if necessary.

Choose labels from a supermarket catalogue. Pick images with small print and enough room around them to wrap your box shape. Or you can just use a cutout label on the front.

Cylindrical beads make cans. Sand the bottoms so they stand up. Use masking tape around the bead to mark off a top and colour with a marker. Add labels with glue. ♥

50 *Mimi* Tray

The Goodies
♥ Scavenge a flat shallow lid anywhere between 4 and 8cm on each side
♥ Scrap of pretty paper

I like these stationery container lids because they have a little rim which looks just like a tray and helps to glue the handles. Sewing needs like pins often come in small clear packs with nice shallow rims, too. Glue paper into lid. Add optional handles. Jewelry hoops cut in half and glued into place make pretty handles. However, a simple glued join won't stand up to rough play. ♥

51 *Minnie* Tray

I hoard old fashioned press lids made from metal. I figure it is only a matter of time before they disappear, and they make terrific dollhouse furniture.

The Goodies
♥ Small metal press lid
♥ Scrap of pretty paper or plastic sheeting that looks like lace.

Cover any writing on the lid with a circle of paper. Glue it into place. If you like, add another circle of lace, a sticker, or a circle of plastic . Done! ♥

Bedroom Basics

Pillows and duvets are made the same way. They are big on charm and softie appeal. Straight sewing only is required, or glue if you like.

52 Baba Pillows

The Goodies
- Fabric
- Stuffing

The Babysteps

I like pillows just a bit smaller than the bed, but it is up to you. For a bed pillow, we might want a finished size of 10 x 7cm.

To make a realistic contrast strip, sew or glue the fabrics together before sewing the pillow as usual.

1 Cut fabric twice the size of the finished pillow plus 1.5cm seam allowance all around.

2 Fold right sides together. Sew two L shaped seams starting at the fold line. Clip corners.

Iron the opening in line with the seam to make it easy to sew. Turn right side out and push the corners out with something like a knitting needle.

4 Fill with stuffing.

5 Hand sew the opening.

2 Sew 2 "L" shaped lines of stitching

What about a ribbon or braid trim? Easy! Glue the trim to the front of the fabric before sewing. The trim usually goes a little way in from one edge of the finished pillow, so mentally take away the seam allowance and think about where you want it to run. And leave a little extra at the edges in case it frays. Then sew your cushion as usual.

Foldline
Fold right sides of fabric together

1 For a 10 x 7cm pillow, begin with a piece of fabric that's 13 x17 cm.

Stuff pillow and stitch closed. Finished!

53 *Babette* *Bedding*

Choose soft fabrics that drape well. The filling should be very soft. My favorite is ordinary batting, because I pull it out into a thin cobwebby layer. It makes a soft but flexible quilt. Or recycle old stockings or T shirt fabric, just keep it thin.

The Goodies
- ♥ Fabric
- ♥ Batting

The Babysteps

1 Start with a long strip of fabric so that when finished, one short edge doesn't have a seam at all. This goes at the bottom of the bed where it is visible from the front of the dollhouse.

Decide on the finished size you want. Don't forget the overhanging sides! I allow 3-4cm for the overhangs on one short side and both long sides. The seam allowance is 1.5cm all around.

Continue Babette by following Babysteps 2 & 3 for Baba Pillows and Cushions, then continue Babette step 4.

4 Pull batting out into a very fine cobwebby layer the same size as the finished quilt. Push into the corners of the quilt. Or use any soft, thin fabric. Foam is much too firm.

5 Hand sew closed.

Want stunningly gorgeous bedding instantly, for less than a dollar? Perfect 1:6 scale blankets are sitting in the supermarket disguised as packs of microfiber cleaning cloths. Ravishing colors, and nicely finished too, in just the kinds of sizes we can use without any work at all. Now that's my kind of project! They can be ironed to flatten them but be a bit careful and start with a cool iron.

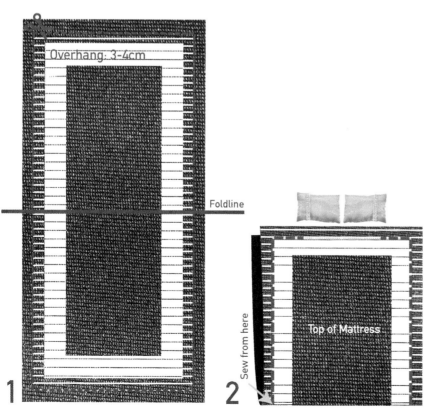

Overhang: 3-4cm

Foldline

Sew from here

Top of Mattress

1

2

54 Babita Mattress

The Goodies

- ♥ Foam or soft fabrics
- ♥ Fabric
- ♥ Glue
- ♥ Hook and Loop dots if needed
- ♥ Cardboard.

The Babysteps

I have a few rules for mattresses.

I usually glue mattresses in place, because otherwise they will probably become another piece of flotsam on the floor. Or use hook and loop adhesive dots for a semi permanent fix.

I like to glue the bottom of the padding to a bed size piece of cardboard before covering, so it stays flat. The cardboard base gives a bit of shape. Without it, they turn into jellyfish-like blobs.

A thin mattress like the one for Bayo bed (p. 56) is just a layer of 5mm foam cut to the size of the base, wrapped on one side with fabric and glued on. It looks pretty nice just the same. A thicker mattress is 3cm foam, treated just the same, with a square edge wrap.

And why not recycle? Soft, fluffy fabrics and clothing are cut to size and folded, glued to a piece of cardboard and covered as usual.

And the cover? Most fabrics work. Pick one that is medium weight. Most cottons and stretch T shirting work well. Fabric should be the size of the mattress plus 2x the depth of the stack plus 3-4cm to turn under. Extra fabric tends to get in the way.

Square edge wrap (see The Basics p. 09) the corners and glue, putting a little bit of pressure on it to keep the fabric tight. Glue the short ends first so the sides will look good. Done!

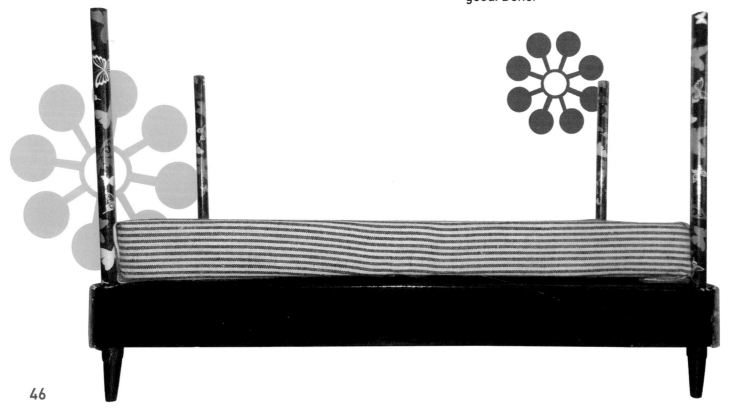

Clockwise from left:
Abby Blinds p. 16, Akiko Lamp p. 31,
Baji Bed, Myra Bottles p. 69, Tori Table p. 30

55 *Baji*
Wooden Box Bed

This is a scavenge project. Your mission is to locate and scavenge the perfect box, and it may be hiding quietly in a corner of a thrift shop, its star potential unrecognized. It might even be sitting on the footpath near your tram stop, for days, like this one. That is, until I couldn't resist anymore, and took it home with me.

The Goodies

A wooden or strong cardboard or plastic box, long enough for a bed. You can be a bit flexible about the length. I like the finished bed to be long enough for the doll to fit on it, more or less. So 25cm long is my minimum. A similar simple box could become a sleek modern bed.

I love the dramatic decoration on this box. Boules come in gorgeous boxes, just the right size, and best of all there are two matching parts, one for the base and one for the head.

The Babysteps

Just unscrew the hinges and voila! Bed base and bedhead. Glue them together as you like, perhaps leaving room each side for a nightstand or shelf. Add some bedding (see Babette p. 45), and done!

47

56 Bambi *Four Poster Bed*

A glamorous four poster is an easy make. What a classic!
And, at last count, I figure it costs less than a dollar to make.

The Goodies

- Shallow box lid: a small shoe box lid is a good size
- Pencils
- Ballpoint pen twist caps
- Glue
- Map pins
- Bling

The only challenge here is making sure that you pick pencils that fit into the pen caps. 5mm pencils usually fit well. So when you are putting the goodies together, check that they are a good fit. And remember that you can sharpen the ends of unsharpened pencils for a better fit into the pen cap.

The Babysteps

1 Make holes at the four corners of the box. Start with a really small hole, with something like small scissors. Don't use a craft knife for this! Then wiggle the pencil through, pointy end down if it is sharpened. If your pencils aren't sharpened, use one that is to make the hole almost big enough.

2 Glue the pen caps from the underside, onto the ends of all 4 pencils. Use plenty of glue.

3 Get ready! We have to get those posts lined up fair and square. The easy way to do this is let the glue job (Step 4) dry with the bed set up around a table corner, with the underside of the bed along one side of the table, and the post along the other. Put some plastic putty in strategic places to hold the bed and support the post while it all dries.

4 Glue bedposts into place. You can use hot glue if you are quick! Otherwise, best use a slower drying glue. Line up the top of the cap to the lower edge of the bed, so that all the legs will be the same. If the post is too far from the corner, add a strip of cardboard into the corner as a filler.

Easy, and no measuring! Run a generous strip of glue inside the corner and hold the pencil against the box and into the corner so it is upright and supported on both sides. Pull the pieces into shape and let it all dry. Repeat with all four posts.

5 Add pushpins to the tops of the pencils. They will push into the lead in the middle quite easily. Earring backings make the gold part of the finial with the map pin pushed straight through.

A bed in minutes! But you might want to add a mattress (Babita p. 46) and some bed linen (Babette p. 45).

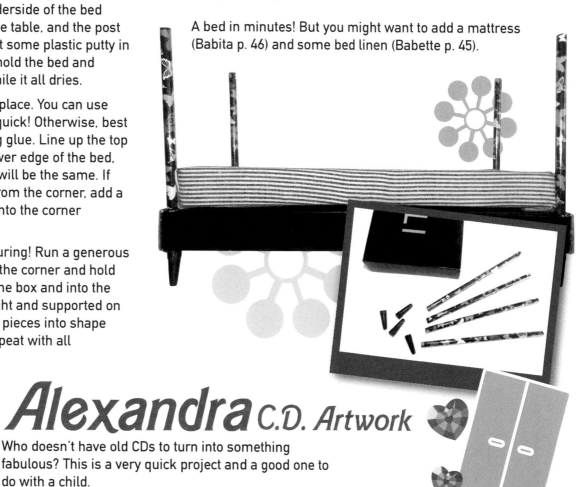

57 *Alexandra* C.D. Artwork

Who doesn't have old CDs to turn into something fabulous? This is a very quick project and a good one to do with a child.

The Goodies
- CDs are light and will stay in place on the wall with hook and loop dots or plastic putty.
- Bling: earrings, stickers, medallions, lace motifs, etc.

The Babysteps

1 Choose some shiny bling to add to our boring CD. I have glued cheap plastic earrings to the middle of the CD. They are mirrored for extra impact, and that is one of the reasons I chose them, of course.

2 We have to do something about the hole in the middle. It shrieks "CD"! Glue some colored paper to match the room behind the central hole in the CD. This shows off the pattern the bling makes through the clear part of the middle of the CD.

Those little mirrors sure do bring a touch of magic to our bedroom!

58 Barbara Wardrobe

Some reworking and a pretty paint job turns a secondhand plywood tissue box into a smart wardrobe, complete with drawers if you like.

Clockwise from left:
Barbara Wardrobe, Miranda Hangers p. 52, Ellie Mirror, Alice Frames p. 52, Annabelle Plants p. 67, Topaz Table p. 25, Suzette Stool

The Goodies

- ♥ Plywood tissue box with sliding lid
- ♥ Stationery packaging or shallow boxes for drawers (optional)
- ♥ Plastic covered coathanger wire
- ♥ Flat beads, bling

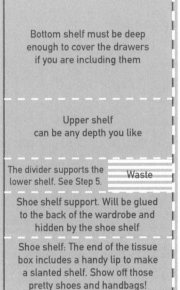

Bottom shelf must be deep enough to cover the drawers if you are including them

Upper shelf can be any depth you like

The divider supports the lower shelf. See Step 5. — Waste

Shoe shelf support. Will be glued to the back of the wardrobe and hidden by the shoe shelf

Shoe shelf: The end of the tissue box includes a handy lip to make a slanted shelf. Show off those pretty shoes and handbags!

Approximate sections for cutting lid. You'll also need to trim a thin strip off the lid lengthwise, to allow shelves to fit snugly into wardrobe

The Babysteps

1 Use the end of the tissue box with the lip for the shoe shelf. Trim to size. Cut the lid to make two shelves, a divider the same depth as the bottom shelf to separate the drawers, and a strip about 2 cm tall to run across the back of the box for the shoe shelf to sit on.

2 Paint except for the shelf support which will be hidden anyway.

3 Glue flat beads to support the upper shelf. Or you can use strips of plywood to support the shelf instead. Glue upper shelf into place.

4 Cut pretty covered coathanger wire for a "rod" and glue into place with a flat bead on either end to help hold it in place.

5 The divider runs front to back under the bottom shelf. It is just higher than the drawers so they will run smoothly and the same depth as the lower shelf. Glue into place. Glue bottom shelf into place. Glue the support strip along the back wall above the bottom shelf and add the shoe shelf.

6 Fill in the oval cutout shape if you like. I cut the oval out of cardboard, glued fabric to it with few tiny pleats to make ruffles, then glued the fabric to the back of the wardrobe. A piece of card glued over the back of the wardrobe covers the lot.

59 Suzette Stool

The Goodies
- Candleholder about 7cm high
- Metal lid: Find a lid that is a tight fit for the top of the candleholder.
- Small piece of padding
- Fabric

The Babysteps

1 Cover the top of the stool with padding and glue into place.

2 Cover padded lid with a fabric circle. Make it big enough to cover the entire lid and turn under. Glue fabric into place on the underside of the lid.

3 Add some more glue and glue lid to candleholder.

60 Ellie Mirror

The Goodies
- Coaster
- Mirror smaller than the coaster
- Self adhesive plastic jewels

The Babysteps

1 Glue mirror to middle of coaster. A real mirror is safe as long as you glue it well.

2 Add crystals in squares around the mirror working from the mirror to the edge.

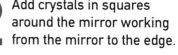

51

61 *Miranda* Hangers

The Goodies
- ♥ Plastic tubing from spray bottle
- ♥ Small screw hooks, preferably the cheap ones
- ♥ Thin wire
- ♥ Fabric

The Babysteps

1 Start with 6.5cm of tubing. Mark the middle of the tube and make a hole . Enlarge it by screwing the hook into it.

2 Cut off half of the screw part of the hook to shorten it (That's why I like the cheap ones. Easier to cut.)

3 If you want a curved hanger, curve a piece of wire just a little shorter than the tubing into shape and push it inside the tubing.

4 Cut a strip of fabric 3 cm wide and 2 cm longer than the hanger. Make a hole in the middle of the fabric for the screw hook. Put a little glue onto the thread of the hook and twist it through the hole in the fabric and into the tubing.

5 Glue fabric strip around the hanger.

6 Cut both ends of the fabric down to 5mm longer than the hanger. Stuff the ends into the tubing with the pointy end of a skewer. Keep going until it makes a neat end. Done.

62 *Alice* Frames
Flat earrings make adorable picture frames.

The Goodies
- ♥ Large hoop or square earrings with a flat back
- ♥ Small picture
- ♥ Sticky jewels
- ♥ Thin cardboard

The Babysteps

1 Cut a cardboard backing a little smaller than the earring and a suitable picture a little smaller again. Glue.

2 Add jewels to cover the hole in the earring. Embellish further if you like. Done!

63 *Bari* Doll Bed

The tiniest household members need a place to sleep too! I remember thinking that my dolls should be put to bed each night and feeling guilty if they were in the cold. I was very young! This is a bed for a doll, or maybe for a tiny furry pet, and it is very easy to make.

The Goodies

- ♥ Tin or basket (look for one with a good shape, oval or rectangular)
- ♥ Pen bits or bead legs 2-3 cm high
- ♥ Paint
- ♥ Decorations if you like
- ♥ Cardboard, padding, fabric (for bedding)

The Babysteps

1 Glue legs to bottom of bed.

2 Paint your bed

3 For the bedding, make an Upholstered Softie Pad to fit inside the bed (see The Basics p. 08). For a mini pet bed, stop right there! Done!

4 Cut fabric for the coverlet, about 2cm bigger all around than the softie pad. Pick a pretty pattern for the coverlet. I used the same fabric as the bunks and chose an oval motif.

5 Turn one end under and glue to make the free edge of the coverlet.

6 Glue edges of coverlet to the underside of the softie pad, leaving it a little loose on the top to hold a doll.

7 Place completed bedding into tin.

8 Add decoration if you like, but it should be quite flat. Anything that juts out will look like a handle.

The T.V. was made from part of a discarded light switch.

53

64 *Baylee* Bunkbeds

Two is more fun. One of the memories that adults often tell me about is playing 'Barbies' with a sister or a best friend for hours at a time. I wanted a project for two children to play together with their dolls, so it had to be big enough and sturdy enough for two.

Obviously we are not going to make this from scratch! That would involve real carpentry. No, no, no...so we upgrade a wooden CD storage unit. Turn it on its side, and Voila! Bunk beds.

CDs boxes are a good size— CDs are about 14 x 12cm, and that is a good size for play between the bunks. The preloved towers are sturdy and dirt cheap, and I think available almost everywhere. When I saw this sturdy CD tower for $2, there was no hesitation. Home it came.

The Goodies

♥ Pick a wooden CD tower that is about 30cm high, just right for a bed when turned on its side.

But, before you buy, check the inside of your tower. We want to be able to pull out the CD holders— that's the plastic pieces that line the inside. It is easy to check that they are held in by little screws and a bit of a tug will show that they are not glued in. The ones I have checked have all been screwed together, and come apart easily, but you never know.

There's a big bonus if you pick the right tower. There is a beautiful railing for the upper bunk, inside the tower, disguised as a boring black plastic CD rack.

The Babysteps

1 First, some demo work. Use a small Phillips head screwdriver to remove the screws holding the plastic racks to the sides of the tower, and out they come.

2 Paint your tower. Pick a great color. A gentle sand is a good idea, but optional unless your wood is very highly polished. Think about making the back wall the same colour as your dollhouse bedroom wall, so that it looks as if the bunks are open.

3 Paint your lovely bonus railing too, if your CD tower had one. Try your paint first, just to make sure it doesn't peel. This is one time I would definitely use an undercoat/primer, because some plastics might not paint well. I have tried a few and they were fine and looked good painted.

4 Glue rail to bunk, leaving at least 7cm above the bunk level so it can be seen above the mattress. Or, use the screw holes and the screws from the demo to hold the railing in place. All you have to do is drill some small holes into the back of the bunk to take the screws.

5 Add flat beads or stickers to decorate as you like.

6 I think quite young children will like to play with Baylee, so I used hook and loop adhesive dots to keep the mattresses in place on the bunks. Ready for our sleepover, Mom!

65 *Bayo* Box Bed

Want a fun project that costs pennies and turns out something precious all the same?

Turn a box into a bed. What could be cheaper or easier than making a fabric strip to go around a freebie box, with or without a mattress? This one definitely earns the Budget Beauty prize.

Will you make the simple bed or add a bedhead? Do you want to make a separate mattress? We will make the simplest version, with some padding on top. But if you want to make a mattress, and it is very easy to do (see Babita Mattresses p. 46), use a shallower box, say 4cm high, so the finished bed will be a nice height.

The Goodies
- ♥ Box
- ♥ Fabric
- ♥ Glue
- ♥ Padding (optional)

This box was a humble display unit at our local hardware store.
I like hardware boxes. They are stronger than grocery boxes because they transport heavier, more expensive items. Frozen pastries come in boxes that are just the right size too.

Bayo is all about the fabric, so inspect your stash and pick the prettiest. And think about the trims. Bayo in a plain fabric demands trims! A horizontal design like a stripe looks good on the valance. Or go very delicate. Mix and match your fabrics to show off your work!

1 Cover top of box

2 Thin Mattress

3 Finish Strip

Clockwise from left:
Aditi Lamp p. 26, Monica Tissue Box p. 63,
Bayo Bed, Baba Pillows p. 44, Babette
Blankets p. 45, Akiko Lamp p. 31

The Babysteps

1 Cover the top of the bed. Cut the fabric a generous 6cm bigger all around. This is not a precision job– the edges will be covered. Square edge the corners (See The Basics p. 09).

2 Cut a thin piece of foam the same size as the top of the bed and cover with fabric. Glue to top of bed.

3 Make a finish strip for a valance (see The Basics p. 08). It should be the height of the bed and long enough to wrap right around and overlap. Turn under the free short end to tidy it up and glue into place. If you are using a supermarket box with a cut edge at the bottom, bring the lower edge of the valance inside the box to conceal the cut edge.

4 (Optional) Fill the box with a stack of pieces of cardboard cut to size. This gives it some extra weight. And for a neat finish, cover the underside of the last piece with matching fabric. Glue all with plenty of glue.

66 *Beatrice* Bedhead

This is such a simple job, and so sweet. It works well with Bedelia Bed Canopy, because the fabric of the drape can be tied to it. Be a bit careful in matching your frame and bed base. It is easiest if the frame is slightly narrower than your bed base so the valance can just wrap around. Plan to use a sturdy bed base because the metal photo frames can be quite heavy.

The Goodies

♥ Frame: I knew as soon as I saw it that this pretty metal frame was a bedhead in disguise, being sold for a measly 50 cents at my lovely local opshop.
♥ Wire
♥ Fabric
♥ Thin padding

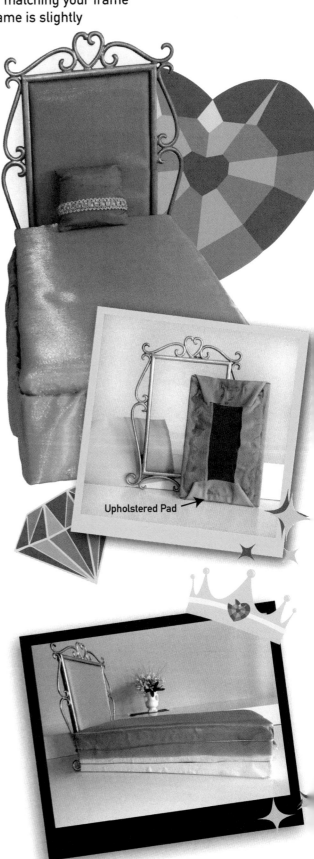

Upholstered Pad

The Babysteps

1 Take out the backing piece as if you are changing the picture.

2 Trace around the back piece and use that for a pattern. Cut a piece of padding the size of the backing piece and a piece of fabric 3cm larger all around.

3 We need the backing piece to fit back into the frame, even with the extra fabric wrapped around it, so sometimes you might have to make the backing piece a little smaller all around. You could sand the edges of a wooden backpiece, or trim cardboard with your craft knife.

Look at your backing piece to see how much room there is before you start. If it is a really tight fit, think about making the backing piece a little smaller if you can. And don't make the padding too big! It should sit neatly without wrapping around to the back.

4 Make an Upholstered Pad (See The Basics p. 08) with the backing piece, padding and fabric. Put pad, and then the backing piece back into the frame. Just like it was before, but without the glass!

5 Attach your adorable new bedhead to the bed base. Glue might not be enough! Wrap two lengths of firm wire to hold the frame to the bed. It needs to go all the way around and twist together with pliers at the back of the bed, tucking the ends of the wires out of the way. You can glue as well, or wrap with tape, making this a very sturdy bed.

67 *Becky*
Ruffled Bed Valance

The Goodies

♥ Cardboard
♥ Fabric
♥ Glue: Hot glue can be lumpy, and it will burn your fingers as you make the ruffles. I use a craft glue.

Pretty fabric and trim dress up a simple box bed (like Bayo p. 56) for major eye appeal. Becky can be bright and cheery or as elaborate as you like.

Ordinary corrugated cardboard is fine for the valance, but make sure the corrugations run up and down on your valance. Otherwise it won't fold around the corners! To make a sharp corner in other kinds of cardboard, score along the fold on the inside.

The Babysteps

1 Cut a strip of cardboard long enough to go exactly around the bed base. It can be almost as high as the box, or much smaller, up to you. If you need to join the cardboard, place the ends side by side and use ordinary tape. The join will be hidden by the fabric anyway.

2 Cut a strip of fabric about one and a half times the length of the cardboard to allow for the ruffles, and 6cm wider for turnover at top and bottom.

3 Match the middle of the fabric to the middle of the cardboard. Use a paperclip to hold the ends in place, leaving enough fabric at both top and bottom to fold under .

4 Starting from the middle (this will be the foot of the bed) put a thin strip of glue along top and bottom of the back of the cardboard, and all over the front. Use a piece of scrap cardboard to spread the glue evenly. Work on 20cm at a time. Pleat the fabric into ruffles and glue to the back, adding extra glue to keep the ruffles in place.

5 Glue the valance to the bed, starting behind the head of your bed where it can't be seen. Glue around the whole bed base, folding at the corners.

Becky is adaptable. Allow for the protruding legs at the bottom of the frame by cutting small rectangles in the cardboard only to let legs peek out. Do this before you cover the cardboard with your fabric. The fabric just flows around the corner. Don't cut the fabric, just the cardboard! This bed now has sweet little legs.

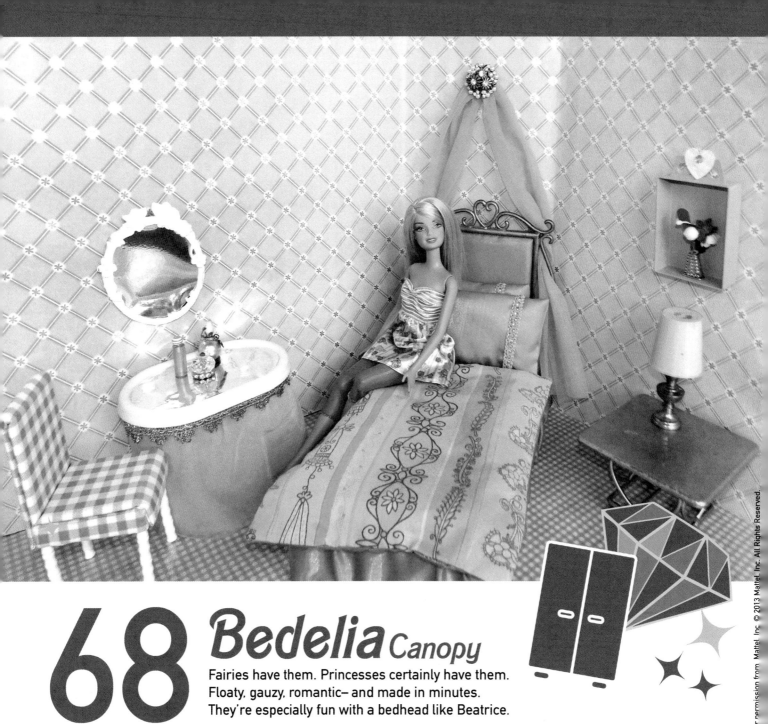

68 *Bedelia* Canopy

Fairies have them. Princesses certainly have them.
Floaty, gauzy, romantic– and made in minutes.
They're especially fun with a bedhead like Beatrice.

The Goodies

- ♥ Small screw hook or screw eye
- ♥ Fabric
- ♥ Bow, button or bead for trim

Pick a fabric that drapes well and doesn't need to be hemmed for a really quick project. Netting, lace, gauze, semi-transparent floaty fabrics look lovely.

The Babysteps

1 Handstitch or glue the trim to outside of hook.

2 Screw hook into wall. For most materials, you will not even need a predrilled hole. The little screw bit will twist straight in. If necessary, make a starter hole, even with a drawing pin!

3 For most fabrics, a strip 8-10cm wide is about right. Extra fabric puffs out and looks clumsy. Pull fabric through hook. Attach to bedhead if you like with wire, needle and thread or glue. Add bows and flowers. Or you can put more screw hooks into the wall close to the bed and push the fabric through.

Cut container base
if necessary

69 *Beena* Dressing Table

A yogurt container with a pretty shape, some fabric and some braid trim.
That's it! A ten minute project, and what a nice one it is. A classic
dressing table, complete with skirt. Oh, is that Mr Hitchcock calling?

The Goodies

- Plastic food container with a tight fitting lid
- Sheer fabric: choose a sheer or lace fabric that doesn't need a hem to simplify the job
- Glue
- Rubber band (optional)

Pick a container with an interesting shape.
I like this yogurt container because it narrows
to the floor and the lid has a stylish curved lip.

The Babysteps

1 Demo Time! If the container is too high,
like this one, cut it down with a craft knife.
It is quite easy to do this, just work on a
hard surface and keep the fingers of your
other hand out of the way. It should be
10-11cm high with the lid on.

2 Cut fabric to twice the height of your tub and fold in two to
make a skirt. It should be one and a half times as long as
the distance around the tub. Start at the back, and glue the
folded fabric to the top of the tub, making small ruffles,
mainly at the front. There is often a neat little ridge at the top
to guide you! Make sure that the lid will still fit back on. For a
really quick fun mini, just use a rubber band instead of glue.
No one will ever know, and the job can be done in minutes!

3 Add some extra weight to Beena if you like, with cut up
cardboard or washers glued inside the container. If you did
cut the container, put the bottom section back inside the
main piece and glue or tape into place.Glue braid trim to
cover the top of the fabric skirt. Put the lid back on.

4 Decorate the top. Paint or glue some paper to fit. Photocopy
the lid to get a good pattern to cut. Makes it easy to get the
right shape when it is not possible to trace it, like this lid
with its deep rim.

70 Tracy Table

Repurpose an adorable candleholder bought for peanuts merely because fashion has moved on. Pick the sweetest you can find, as long as it has enough flat surface at the top to glue to a topper into place.

The Goodies

- Pretty candleholder, 5-6cm high for a side table
- Topper: A coaster, shallow lid, or box top.
- Small lengths of skewer if your base is like this one, and doesn't have much flat surface at the top.

The Babysteps

1 Glue topper to candle-holder. Glue skewer lengths on the inside of the join for some extra strength.

2 Paint and done!

Another option! Use silver paper and stick on jewels to match Bernice Styling Station (p 68).

71 Bekka
Wall Shelf

The Goodies

Scavenge a small shallow box or lid, probably plastic, but the lid of a small tin or a cardboard box would also work. Mine is made from packaging. It held paperclips and cost, including the contents, precisely $1 at the import store. Containers like this also make neat drawers at 1:6 scale (see Barbara Wardrobe p. 50).

These boxes are 70x55mm. I like them because they have a hanger that can be a hanging rail, or turned the other way to make a topper detail for a traditional look.

The Babysteps

1 Paint your shelf. A transparent box like this can be painted on the inside. A pretty paper on the back looks good, too.

2 Add some bling to the top and glue into place. The topper is just a button, complete with its shank at the back. But if you need to, you can usually cut the shanks off buttons.

Try scavenge finds, or use a variation of the bead leg (see Chapter 2, The Basics p.08) for the base.

72 *Allegra* Lamp

The Goodies

- ♥ Disposable small glass or small container for shade
- ♥ Lid and wand from lip gloss or mascara packaging
- ♥ Flat sided bead or cork circle

The Babysteps

1 Paint the inside of the plastic small glass. They are fun to paint– you can hold the outside and not get your fingers dirty. This is easy for a child to do, with instant results!

2 Cut off brush/applicator from the wand and push a bead or cork circle onto the cut end. Adjust length and glue.

3 Glue stand into shade.

73 *Monica* Tissue Box

The Goodies

- ♥ Small cardboard box: This one is a lipstick box. A ring box is also a good size.
- ♥ Scrap of tissue

The Babysteps

1 Cut box to size.

2 Strengthen the inside with some adhesive tape.

3 Make a small slit in the top with a craft knife

4 Push tissue through.

Make the bottles on the table on p. 69!

74 *Belinda* Bedhead

Hmmm...how to make a traditional carved bedhead without tools and without any woodworking skills at all? Obviously we have to use the bits and pieces the universe has supplied for us.

The Goodies

- ♥ Plywood
- ♥ Round wooden coaster: They are usually about 9cm diameter
- ♥ Ordinary wooden clothes pegs
- ♥ Bling and paint

The Babysteps

The coaster makes a curved top and the pegs add carved detail at the sides. Pick a nicely finished peg, because some are neater than others! Pick two that are similar– they vary quite a lot.

We can cut plywood with a craft knife, or use a picture frame back or scavenged piece of thin wood for the backing piece. It needs to be wide enough to glue the coaster and pegs on with a bit of space in between, so about 11-12cm wide. Mine is 15cm high. Match to your bed, and add bling as you wish.

1 Test the pieces together with a little plastic putty. Mark the level of the top of the mattress. Also mark the middle of your backing piece to center the coaster.

2 Glue coaster to backing piece so it will sit just above the mattress. This leaves a flat area to glue to the bed later.

3 Separate the peg into two pieces by slipping them off the metal spring. The spring just pulls out.

4 Glue the half pegs into place along the outside edges of the backing piece. The peg can meet the top of the backing piece or a little higher if you like.

5 Paint. Add bling.

75 *Beltane* Necktie Upholstered Bed

Silk, upholstered luxury and gorgeous colors.
For less than a dollar. Who knew?

Ordinary neckties have a long padded strip at the narrow end and it just so happens that it is usually long enough to go around our beds at 1:6 scale. The wide part of the tie makes a bunch of cushions. Have a mixy-matchy scheme for a few pennies! The world is full of pretty ties!

The Goodies

- Suitable box bed, block of wood, or artist's canvas
- Pretty tie
- Stuffing
- Extra fabric

This works really well with a box the same depth as the tie. And a cheap artist's canvas makes a sturdy bed.

The Babysteps

1 Cover the top surface of your box with padding if you like.

2 Using the extra fabric, cover top and sides of bed using square edge corners (see The Basics p. 09). Bring the fabric down the side of the box so that the tie will cover the edges.

3 Glue the a strip of the tie right around the box, just as it is. Start behind the head of the bed so the join will be hidden. Glue the ready made V shape over the cut end. Instant upholstery, and it takes about 2 minutes! That is a really quick mini.

4 We can neaten the lower edge of the box with a tiny bit more work. Undo the stitching at the center of the tie back. Ties are held together at the back by a few very loose stitches. They almost fall apart.

Then unfold the top flap. That top flap always has a neat folded hem already made for us! Easy! Leave it as it is. It can tuck under the edge of a cardboard box, to give it a custom look.

5 Making pillows from ties: The only thing to be aware of when using ties is the bias. The bias is the way the fabric runs. We want to cut our cushions on the straight of the fabric, so we cut at the same angle as the V at the bottom of the tie (See the photo). We do not cut straight across the tie, oh nonono, because that will give us pieces cut on the bias, and they will stretch and look really odd. Otherwise, follow the instructions for Baba (p. 44).

76 Berit *Platform Bed*

This platform bed is really fun to make. It looks good alone, or with any headboard. Berit is a platform bed, with a glam painted surrounding ledge, so we make the mattress smaller than the frame.

The Goodies

♥ This is a scrounge and scavenge project. Just look for the right kind of picture frame! It has to be long enough to make a bed so at least 25cm long, and have a flat surface at the front. Mine was painted silver, so I haven't even repainted it!

♥ Two wooden blocks, about 4cm high, at least 5cm shorter than the width of the frame to be the supports.

The Babysteps

1 Remove the extras. We only use the frame and the wooden or cardboard backing piece. Remove the glass, the picture, the prop stand, any fittings for hanging, etc. Just pull out the little nails (brads) that hold the wire with a claw hammer or pliers. Most frames this shape will be for hanging, and won't have a prop at all. Some props are just glued on and come off easily. The ones with annoying black rivets are pretty tough, and pulling them off will probably damage the backing piece. Fortunately, it doesn't matter. No one will ever know!

2 Glue the backing piece into the frame— just as it was, only it won't be removable any more.

3 Fill the front of the picture space with cardboard, padding or even old towelling. We want to make a level surface to put the mattress on.

4 Make a mattress to fit the frame (see Babita mattresses p. 46).

5 Glue the blocks to the underside (back) of the frame. Place one support at the head of the bed in line with the edge of the frame to make it stable. Place the support at the foot end of the bed set in a little from the edge of the frame so the bed "floats.".

Clockwise from left:
Berit Bed, Babette Bedding p. 45, Allegra
Lamp p. 63, Myra Bottles p. 69, Annabelle
Plants, Bernice Styling Station p. 68,
Bekka Wall Shelf p. 62

77 *Annabelle*
Flowers & Plants

The Goodies
- Artificial plant materials, as small as you can get
- Upcycled container lids, small jars, beads, lids, etc.
- Glue
- Clear nail polish
- Bonsai granite or tiny pebbles

It is quite hard to find flowers small enough for 1:6 scale. I stayed with the flowers that seem to be easy to get. Mini roses are always available at craft and fabric stores. Fake gypsophila (the little white ones) and spiky green stalks I can usually find at the import stores. I think the purple buds are lilac, but it cuts down into something that looks like spring bulbs.

Containers can be anything that has a hole or can have a hole drilled in it. Many beads have tiny holes, only big enough for a string, so unless you want to have a go at drilling a larger hole, choose carefully.

The Babysteps
Hot glue is great for a quick job. Fill container with glue, arrange flowers and glue. Done.

At this scale, stalks have to be short to look right. Be prepared to cut your flowers down a lot. For flowerpots, the flower should be close to the rim. And you can trim spikes down lengthwise to make them thinner.

The curly white 'flowers' are cut from the end of a full size bunch. The container is a lipstick lid. The whole thing is so light that it falls over all the time! So add a weight to the bottom if needed. Bonsai granite mixed with some clear nail polish is a high fashion way to hold flowers in a clear vase.

Scavenge twigs and place in a small bottle. Very dramatic!

78 Bernice
Styling Station

The Goodies
- 3 shallow clear lids for a backing, tabletop and support
- Silver paper
- Strips of plastic jewels

Choose a shallow lid for the back piece. This one was from a chocolate box. I liked the way this lid formed a little alcove. The backpiece needs to be at least 17 cm high.

Small clear packaging items make the table top and support. For the table, choose a little flat surface. Perhaps a lid, or a shallow box. The support makes the whole thing stable and needs to be deeper. This was the container for my dressmaking pins!

The Babysteps

1 Cut paper to cover the top of the table, the front of the support and to make the mirror. Glue into place.

2 Glue the support and table top together in a T-shape with the silver side of the support facing the front. The table top will join the backpiece. Position it so that there will be some leg room for our doll.

3 Then glue the back of the tabletop to the backpiece.

4 Bling is fun for this one. Stick it on the top of the backpiece, on the table edge, the pedestal and so on. I have used stick on diamantes, which are self adhesive and take only seconds to cut to size. And they fill in any inconvenient gaps in our beautiful finished project.

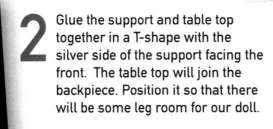

Make Suzette Stool on p. 51!

79 *Myra*
Perfume Bottles

The Goodies
- ♥ Beads
- ♥ Glue
- ♥ Push pins/ Dressmaking pins
- ♥ Imagination!

You can make enough pretty bottles for a beauty salon in one sitting. And you'll use up some of those precious bits of saved bling.

Perfume bottles can be as extravagant as you like. Have a look at real ones for inspiration! Small gold and silver beads make nice tops, flat buttons and beads make jars. Sweet buttons often come with annoying shanks on the back, but they are easily cut off with your trusty pliers to make either lids or pots. Clear buttons make neat jars. Map pins make good round lids and hold the rest together too.

Lots of beads will not stand up. They were designed to hang around necks, not to take pride of place in a dollhouse. But most can be sanded so that they will stand up. Use coarse paper and put it flat on a worktop. Then gently sand the bead, holding it straight up at 90°. Once it stands up, stop sanding! This works, honest! I have done it lots of times. Even with glass and ceramic beads.

Having trouble getting a nice straight bottle? Use a long pin to connect the beads with dabs of glue between them. The head of the pin can make the top of the bottle for an easy mini, or use a dressmaking pin to hide the fixing. Tweak and then leave it all alone! Let the glue dry.

80 *Blair* Vanity

The Goodies

- ♥ Box 10-12cm tall
- ♥ Drawer liner or paper for vanity front
- ♥ Small white bowl

The boxes that coasters come in are ideal, but adapt freely with whatever you can find. About 10cm tall is a good height.
Drawer liner roll makes an inexpensive, interesting vanity front.
Translucent vinyl works for both vanity and shower screen.
The little dipping sauce bowls from Asian stores make adorable trendy handbasins.

The Babysteps

The handy little grooves in the sides of the box hold our smart new front in place

1 Cut cardboard and drawer liner to fit in the same way the sliding box lid would. Or glue in to place.

2 Glue basin to middle of box top.

Blair

Bo

Blythe

81 *Blythe*
Toilet

The Goodies
♥ Vaseline container or a similar container
♥ Dental floss or mini mint holder for cistern

First the bad news: There is no easy way to make a lifelike toilet at this scale. The good news? Toilets come in lots of shapes nowadays. Which is an excellent thing for dollhouse decorators, because the old "S" bend was impossible to fake. The other good news? A very common jar from any supermarket makes a pretty good modern toilet, with a routine paint job. "Vaseline" comes in an oval plastic container with smooth lid. It is a good size and the shape is perfect.

My tip? Place it narrow end facing out into the room, to disguise the lack of plumbing.

The Babysteps
Paint as usual, and start with a primer. Don't sand. No need to paint the backs. Glue toilet and cistern to wall and floor. Done!

82 *Bo*
Toilet Roll Holder

The Goodies
♥ Spring from clothes peg
♥ Bead
♥ Tissue

The spring just slides out from the clothes peg. The bead needs to have at least one flat surface and holes suitable for the wire

The Babysteps
Cut about 15cm of tissue the width of the spring. In this case, 1cm wide. Attach to spring with a square of tape, and wind onto spring to look like toilet paper. Push the ends of the spring into the holes of the bead, and glue to wall.

83 *Bobbie* Shower

We are going to have a very simple shower with a screen.

The Goodies
- Lightweight picture frame
- Semi opaque drawer liner (the same as we used for Blair vanity.)

Pick a frame with some interesting detail to make a screen, preferably plastic, metal or resin, and with flat edges so it will stand up.

The Babysteps

Discard everything except the frame, because we want light to come through. Paint frame on both sides. Cut liner to fit the hole and glue in place in the back of the frame Double sided tape can be good for this. Glue to floor and wall. If you want to keep your screen removable, you can make a unit by gluing it to the toilet or vanity so the whole thing will stand on its own.

84 *Brenna* Towel Rack

The Goodies
- Length of coat hanger wire: 8-10cm is good, but tailor to size
- Two beads: Must have at least one flat side and holes suitable for the wire.

The Babysteps

Glue wire into holes, keeping the flat sides of the beads facing the same way. Glue flat sides to wall. (The towel is cut from a microfiber cleaning cloth).

85 Bridget
Bathtub

The Goodies
♥ Long rectangular or oval dish

The Babysteps
My favorite bath is a long flat food storage container, at least 18 x 6cm inside, so the doll can sit upright in it. The lids always split or get lost, but the containers are very sturdy, and can be painted or decorated with stickers, adhesive paper or tape. If you can find one that is already white, bingo!

Bathing dolls is a very popular activity. If your tub will see active duty, decoration should go on the outside! Use a primer for the first coat, paint the rim and have a wet rag handy to keep wiping paint from the inside. Most baths are white these days, but adjust your palette as fashion dictates. Glue to floor if you like.

If yours is a working dollhouse, serious hydro action is inevitable, so accept that there will be wear and tear, and keep hunting for that perfect bath.

86 Britney
Taps

The Goodies
♥ Coat hanger wire
♥ Beads or bead caps with holes to match wire
♥ L hooks
♥ Buttons and beads, carefully selected
♥ Small washers
♥ Top of talc package or large flat bead for showerhead

The Babysteps
The tap handles are all the same and made from buttons, beads or washers. Ordinary hardware washers make perfect backplates for taps. Glue to wall and add a silver button on top.

Bead caps conceal the join between tap and wall or vanity.

The tall vanity tap is an L hook from the hardware store. Add a bead cap if you like, to conceal the join between the countertop and tap.

The shower head is the top of a talc bottle, with ready made holes! The talc top is made of thin metal so glue a square bead inside with hole facing up, and push wire into that. Bend the wire at a good angle for your room. Drill a hole in the wall the same size as the wire. Glue wire into it, with a bead cap to hide the join between the wall and wire.

A flat silver button with 4 holes makes an outflow for the shower floor, bath or basin.
Just glue into place.

Britney

Bobbie

Britney

Bridget

Index

Made in the USA
Monee, IL
06 December 2020